SAVED
FROM
BANKRUPTCY

The Story of the Boatbuilding Meloons

By

DAVID AND DOROTHY ENLOW

MOODY PRESS
CHICAGO

Contents

Foreword

Many interesting and dramatic success stories have been told by and about men and women in the business world. None, perhaps, has more practical impact and spiritual dynamic than that of the Meloon family in Orlando, Florida, with their unique ministry in near bankruptcy.

Actually, under ordinary circumstances the two words seem contradictory: *success* and *bankruptcy*. And of course, they are. But this is no ordinary story. Ask the hundreds of financially reeling businessmen and missionaries to whom the Meloons have had a spiritual ministry, both in and out of our evangelistic crusades.

Tools for evangelism abound: medical work, tracts, social concern, and many others. But rarely do we consider financial disaster as such a tool, and one of the most effective, at that.

True believers spend a lifetime learning from their mistakes, confessing and forsaking their sins. Then God gives them a vital ministry in helping others who face similar testings and trials. Such counsel—the voice of experience—becomes invaluable to those who hear.

Because he has a Spirit-led and Spirit-filled message to share, Correct Craft President Walt Meloon has been used in a number of our evangelistic crusades, both in this country and abroad. God has been pleased to communicate a vital message through him to individual businessmen as well as groups, both large and small. His two brothers, Ralph and Harold, and his elderly parents, similarly blessed of the Lord, also have shared a vital message with many others in their own effective ways.

In God's economy, the shattering financial crises of the boatbuilding Meloons have been enriching experiences allowed for a very real purpose. That purpose is being realized today in a unique way, in both a gloriously practical and deeply spiritual manner.

All of us probably have experienced, or are experiencing, bankruptcy in one form or another—if not financial, then perhaps physical, spiritual, or social. This book will tell you how others were led by the Lord out of their predicament. Then the joy of the Lord will indeed be your strength as you find a way out of your own problem.

BILLY GRAHAM

6

Introduction

Walter Oswald Meloon (Walt to his many friends),
oldest of three sons of the boatbuilding W. C. Meloon
family, echoed the sentiments of the entire clan when he
said to the authors at the outset of work on this book:
"We want to be very sure no one but the Lord receives
any glory from this book."

It is still true that God uses people to accomplish His
purposes, and that of course necessitates a recital of His
use of this particular family segment of His body. But we
have made every effort to attribute honor only to the
Lord for all that He has done in and through this remarkable family.

They are remarkable, not because they are faultless,
extremely gifted, or nationally known, but rather because they have weathered countless trials and troubles
and tribulations with God's help and have come out
"more than conquerors." Others have done the same
thing in different ways, but few if any have had a
"ministry in bankruptcy," that is, in helping hundreds
of businessmen across the country—and missionaries
on the field as well—to find a satisfactory solution to
their financial woes.

The Meloons are human, with weaknesses like any
and all of God's saints, but through their humanness
shine such things as love, concern, compassion. Much
of our conversation with the Meloons contained many
famous names. But the name they mention most often is

tnat of the Lord Jesus Christ; friend and "foe" alike acknowledge the fact. Would that we could be as faithful in recognizing Him as Lord and Master of our lives.

We came away from our hours and days with the Meloons tremendously blessed, inspired, challenged, and grateful to God for men who first of all want others to know their Lord; men who demonstrate "love in action" by their enthusiasm in serving the Lord, in giving a cup of cold water in His name, in giving of themselves, their time, their means to show they care because their Christ cares. They are men who have learned a proper sense of values and priorities. And we use the word men generically in this instance, for one must certainly include the Meloon women, the elderly Mrs. W. C. Meloon and all of the Meloon wives who have worked alongside their husbands, sharing in their woes and successes, defeats and victories.

When any member of the Meloon family describes personal accomplishments or those of Correct Craft, Inc., you quickly learn they are not interested in personal glory but rather in attesting to the great faithfulness of their heavenly Father, who has brought them through much difficulty to the present time. You cannot be around any member of the family very long before you realize that Christ is not a Sunday religion for them but a week-long, everyday, every moment Person who is their constant Companion and Guide.

1

Crossing the Rhine

In the early months of 1945, General Dwight D. ("Ike") Eisenhower and his Allied forces succeeded almost too well with their military tactics. They moved forward steadily in France, then suddenly found themselves advancing toward Berlin more quickly than they had planned. A logistical problem resulted. Weeks ahead of schedule, they approached the banks of the Rhine River without a sufficient supply of boats to effect a safe crossing.

Eisenhower assessed the military situation, then earmarked March 10 as the most favorable date to cross the river. He knew that he faced a crucial loss of men and time unless he quickly hurdled this greatest obstacle between the Allies and Berlin. His armies would lack supplies and ammunition; they must act in a hurry.

Cabling an SOS to Washington, Eisenhower asked for a March 5 delivery of 569 storm boats to the banks of the Rhine. He needed these compact seventeen-foot vessels because they had spoon-shaped bows constructed so that men could run right over them. Tailor-made for just such maneuvers, the highly expendable boats could skid right up onto beaches at full throttle.

Ike's suppliers could not delay; it was early February

already, and the Allies' strategic gains could be lost unless they pressed their advantage. U.S. Army Engineers quickly responded to the emergency. They began contacting boatbuilders in various parts of the country. High on the list was the Pine Castle Boat and Construction Company in central Florida, a familiar landmark in that area.

The boat company had shut down that February 9 in honor of a friend of the firm for whom funeral services were being held in a little church nearby. Walter C. Meloon (hereafter referred to as W. C. Meloon to avoid confusion with sons and grandsons) left the service with his three sons, Walter, Ralph, and Harold. When they returned to the plant, the watchman handed W. C. a message.

Army engineers had been trying to reach him all afternoon, calling from a district office in Jacksonville, a division office in Atlanta, and the chief's office in Washington, D. C.

When the senior Meloon contacted his caller, the chief engineer explained Eisenhower's situation to him. Then he asked: "How many storm boats can you build by February 28, with a triple-A preference rating and all the cooperation possible from the U.S. Engineers?"

Meloon promised to reply after he held a family conference. What he really wanted was a time of prayer, a necessity before he would make any major decision. Their normal February schedule called for the building of forty-eight boats. How many could they trust the Lord for in this national emergency? How big was their faith? They finally committed the company for 300 storm boats—an impossible task, friends assured them. Yet, they had confidence in God's ability to do the impossible as they did their part.

"We knew we couldn't do it without help from the Lord," the boat executive said.

Next day, Saturday, February 10, the whole plant geared up for the increased production. The Meloons and their employees worked until midnight building jigs—open frames for holding work and guiding machine tools to the work—and making preliminary plans prior to starting production. After stopping to rest on Sunday, they resumed work at 1 A.M. Monday. That day they increased their crew from sixty employees to 320.

Problems multiplied with scarcity of material, priority-plagued transportation, new and inexperienced help, and shortage of time. Army engineers sent help as they had promised: a plant engineer, a staff of inspectors, auditors, material, and labor expediters. Still, only fifteen days remained to complete 300 boats.

Trucks and airplanes traveled all over the United States in search of material to keep production going. Many times the equipment arrived just as supplies gave out. Some of the truck drivers traveled over mountainous roads when storms raged so fiercely that no other vehicles appeared on the road. God carried them through without an accident, which the Meloons considered an answer to prayer.

The expediters offered many suggestions, most of them good. One of them, however, called for a seven-day workweek in view of the urgency involved. The Meloons responded with a polite but firm no.

"We intend to do the job to the glory of God," the senior Meloon said. "It's not His plan to work seven days a week."

The expediter argued that they needed the three extra days to accomplish the task. Explaining why they did not intend to work on Sundays, the Meloons quoted Scripture: "Remember the sabbath day, to keep it holy" (Ex 20:8). "Them that honour me I will honour" (1 Sa 2:30).

"If you insist," they said, "you can have the contract back. This job is impossible for man to do alone."

The Meloons stuck to their guns, even though they knew a possible legal battle with the government might wipe them out. Finally relenting, the engineers gave them permission to work only six days a week on the emergency job.

Similar conflicts arose at their other plant in Titusville, where the Meloons built boats for the navy, including plane-rearming boats, navy whaleboats, and plane personnel boats. Government policy restricted the awarding of contracts to builders from more than one branch of the service at a time. Providentially, the Meloons believe, contracts came from the army and navy on the same day, and remained in effect with government approval.

A navy inspector told the Meloons they could not take time out for weekly chapel services. The boatbuilders again responded firmly.

"If we can't serve the Lord and the U.S. Navy at the same time, we just won't serve the navy."

The navy commander in Jacksonville finally realized the unyielding stand of the Meloons and overruled his subordinate.

"You won't have any further problem with the inspector on this," he assured them.

On Monday, February 12, the company built one storm boat. What seemed like an agonizingly slow process improved so that they built three boats on Tuesday and seven on Wednesday. Some of their own employees shook their heads in disbelief when the Meloons called a halt for the midweek chapel service in the plant. With three of the fifteen days gone, only eleven boats had been built.

That night the Meloon family met together for prayer. They prayed more desperately than ever before, asking God to show them how to do the job. Walt, the oldest son, awakened the next morning with an idea that would speed up production. A new machine and one change on the jig would do the trick. He made the change on the jig.

Ralph located a man who felt he could build the new machine. He required the rest of the week to complete the work. Meanwhile, production accelerated with the change on the jig.

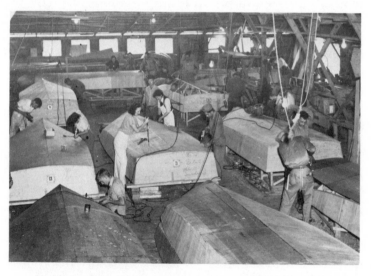

In 1944, Pine Castle plant workers rushed an order for General Dwight D. Eisenhower. The "miracle production" resulted in the delivery of 400 boats ahead of schedule.

13

On Thursday, February 15—less than two weeks from their deadline—the workers built thirteen boats; on Friday, seventeen; Saturday, twenty-one. Still, with six of the fifteen days gone, only sixty-two of the 300 boats had been built.

The work crew rested again on Sunday, then resumed production early Monday morning, February 19. Refreshed by the day of rest and with the new machine in action, they moved ahead at a rapid pace.

On Wednesday, February 21, an army officer flew down from Atlanta. He marveled as he saw boats stacked all over the place. Even the highway in front of the plant had been blocked off, with village, county, and state approval, to accommodate the overflow. The plant hummed with activity. By now the 320 men and women workers were building up to forty-two boats a day.

A local minister presided at the midweek chapel service. He invited the colonel to say a few words to the employees. Standing atop a cutting bench in the middle of a blocked-off Florida highway, the officer looked down into the faces of the workers.

"Men and women," he said, "you have done a remarkable job and I want to compliment you. I have just visited three other plants in the north where they are working on this same job, and all of them together are not doing what you are doing."

Buoyed by the encouraging remarks and a conviction that God was working, the Meloons and their co-workers returned to their task with new zeal.

At noon on Saturday, February 24, a jubilant crew of boatbuilders stood on the sidetrack and saw an express train haul away the 306th boat. The army engineer in charge of the special project said, "There goes our quota four days ahead of schedule. Someone other than man did this job. If it had rained only one day, we couldn't have accomplished it."

A day earlier, the Meloons had received a special request from the chief of engineers. Would they build another hundred boats, as the other three contractors had fallen short of their quota? The Meloons, their accelerated operation now in full swing, delivered 400 boats ahead of time.

On March 2, the same labor expediter who had urged the Pine Castle Boat and Construction Company to work seven days a week, returned to the plant. He stood in front of the shop, tears glistening on his cheeks.

"You folks certainly have faith in the Lord," he said. "I want to congratulate you." Then he shook hands with the senior Meloon and his three sons and walked away.

After presenting the army and navy "E" award to the plant in a special ceremony on May 23, 1945, the government listed the boatbuilding achievement on their records in Washington as "the miracle production."

Visitors from all parts of the United States, for many weeks thereafter. came to see the place where a company could build 400 boats in fifteen days without infringing on the Lord's Day. The Meloons attributed all honor to the God who had led and strengthened them.

"To us," they said, "it was simply an indication that the Lord honors the obedience of His children." He had done it many times before; He certainly would do it again. But, for the Meloons, not without dark days and darker days.

Pretty aquamaids are towed by a Correct Craft boat in their daily performance at Cypress Gardens.

2

Beautiful Cypress Gardens

"Here they come, ladies and gentlemen," barked the voice over the loudspeaker, "the lovely mermaids of Cypress Gardens!"

Six tanned, lithe young girls, their skis atilt, took off behind two speeding white boats across the sparkling water. As they turned and posed on their skis, right hands waving in unison, the crowd applauded, thoroughly enjoying the beautiful scenery, flower-perfumed air, and skillful performance.

Walt Meloon had seen the show many times before. Now he sat in the stands waiting for an appointment with entrepreneur Dick Pope, Sr., founder of Cypress Gardens and promoter extraordinary. Each time tall, graying Walt saw these performers using Correct Craft boats, he experienced the feeling of wonder at what God had done for the whole family of Meloons.

Yes, he reflected, God had been good to a household that moved to Florida from New Hampshire and began a boat business in 1925. They had come a long way since their early years as the Florida Variety Boat Company, the first name given to the struggling family business.

Just think, Walt mused now as he watched the skiers in their intricate maneuvers, *a king—a real live king*

—performed his first water skiing behind a Correct Craft Tournament Skier (a 20-foot water-skiing boat built especially for Cypress Gardens) right here in this beautiful place. Now that same ruler, King Hussein of Jordan, owns three or four of our boats.

Even a Japanese businessman saw this show and bought two used Nautiques. He liked them so well that he urged his friends and business associates to buy more from us, and today we do a good business in Japan.

Tourists from far and wide filled the Marine Stadium and cheered the magnificent precision of the world-famous ski troupe. They laughed at the clowns, and gasped as the kite-flier soared to a height of 300 feet, then released his towline and glided to the beach below.

Water skiers at Cypress Gardens, Florida, make good use of Correct Craft boats in their activity.

An eleven-man human pyramid, the aquamaid ballet, barefoot skiing—all enhanced by the trim boats —tended to make the half hour seem but a fleeting moment for the audience.

"And now," the voice announced, "here are the lovely aquamaids behind the beautiful eighteen-foot Ski-Nautique boats from Correct Craft in Orlando" (better known, of course, than nearby Pine Castle where the plant is located).

The Meloons could hardly have found a better place to show off their boats than Cypress Gardens. They like to bring visiting friends to the exotic spot. When Al Wheeler, a linguist for Wycliffe Bible Translators, brought Chief Ricardo Yaiguaje, his wife, Delores, and his brother Estanislao to Correct Craft in 1965 on their first visit to the United States from their Siona Indian tribe in Colombia, South America, the Meloons took them to the gardens.

After the visiting trio had seen the show, the Meloons presented them with a fiberglass Play'n'Ski boat and smiled as the grateful chief thanked them profusely for the "fire canoe that flies." Ricardo suggested the boat might be used for a bathtub, a modern convenience he had seen for the first time only three days earlier.

Now, after the exciting water show, Walt stifled a nagging sinus cough as he walked briskly to Dick Pope's memento-filled office. The two men discussed their business, then Dick—still active in his mid-70s—leaned back in a reminiscent mood. His rough exterior and snowy white hair belied his flamboyant manner and ready smile.

"I remember the first time I saw your dad," Pope recalled, chuckling as he began his story. "I had ridden to a little town near Winter Haven. Out on one of the

Dick Pope (*left*), founder of Cypress Gardens, is shown receiving a boat from W. C. Meloon.

small lakes, not more than four acres in size, I heard the loudest noise I had heard in a long, long time. A lot of little boats zoomed around the lake. There was your dad maneuvering that thing he called a 'Punkinseed' around the turns with the greatest of ease. He made the other boats look sick. His brother Cal was riding with him."

Pope shifted only slightly as he continued. His smile turned off and on in the mood of the moment. "I asked your dad how much he wanted for one of his boats. As I remember, he charged me $50, and he made sure I paid right away! Since that time, I've had probably every boat company in the world at my door and have tried many of their products. You know, Walt, as far as boats are concerned, it's always been Correct Craft for me."

Dick Pope keeps about $35,000 worth of the Meloon-built boats on hand at all times. In their more than thirty-five years of association, Cypress Gardens and the boatbuilders have never had a written agreement between them, so trusting is their relationship.

Top officials of the Pine Castle firm make the 100-mile round trip often to deliver the Cypress Garden boats or pick them up for service and repairs. It might be the President, Walt Meloon, his Indian-like profile softened by a warm smile; the short, bespectacled vice-president, Ralph Meloon; tall, somewhat heavier Harold Meloon, since 1974 part-time consultant and chaplain; or Walt's thirty-six-year-old son, vice-president and general manager Walter N. Meloon, often called Walt, Jr., who towers above them all at six feet four inches.

As Walt left Dick Pope's office that sunny afternoon, and started the familiar drive back to Orlando, he continued to reminisce. He remembered clearly hearing all about those early struggles of the boating business from Mom and Dad and other members of the family.

Pictured are (*left to right*) Walter C. Meloon's father, Walter Nathaniel Meloon; his aunt Nellie and uncle Joe Meloon, and his uncle Charles Meloon.

The children of Walter Nathaniel Meloon held a reunion in 1919 at Province View Farm, Effingham, New Hampshire, overlooking Province Lake on the Maine border. Walter C. Meloon is second from the left.

3

A Boating Business Is Born

Two families, the Meloons and the Hamms, lived near each other in the small village of Ossipee, New Hampshire. They became warm friends. They belonged to the same church, and the children attended the same school. As the older offspring reached their teens, two of them—Walter Crawford Meloon and Marion Adiena Hamm—began to show more interest in each other.

Walter dropped out of high school after two years and went to work in a little print shop that advertised Mr. Hamm's business, the Balm-Elixir Company, which made a patent medicine liniment. (In its strong formula it became a horse liniment. The weaker solution was intended for people.)

Walter frequently walked home with Mr. Hamm and stayed for supper. One evening, while helping Marion with the dishes, he asked her to marry him. She said she couldn't unless he became a Christian. She had accepted Christ as her Saviour a couple of years earlier and knew that Christians should not be "unequally yoked together with unbelievers" (2 Co 6:14).

Walter responded, "I have become a Christian, and I'll make a public profession as soon as I can." (At the time, their church was closed for lack of a pastor.)

23

The happy couple heard wedding bells a short time later and moved to Buffalo, New York, in 1925. Walter worked first with the Hooker Chemical Company in Niagara Falls and later in St. Catherines, Ontario, helping with the construction of a high-level bridge. He then worked with his older brother, Nat, who operated a foundry, Buffalo Bronze Die Casting Corporation. The company manufactured the big gear for the Ford Model T one-ton truck before the Detroit motor firm began to make its own gears.

Later, Nat, Jr., and his brother Hank followed in their father's footsteps and operated the Meloon Bronze Foundry in Syracuse, New York. They manufactured struts, rudders, and water gear for Correct Craft boats until they sold the company in 1972.

Walter, meanwhile, confronted his spiritual condition early in his married life. He had promised Marion he would settle the matter at the earliest opportunity. Evangelist Lee Aldrich held meetings for a week in Niagara Falls, and one night W. C. went forward. He made a public commitment, was baptized, and later joined the Baptist church. He began to take his living for Christ seriously.

About a week after his public profession, he hammered his thumb instead of a nail and swore. Immediately overwhelmed with guilt and shame, he asked God's forgiveness and help to keep him from doing that again. God answered his prayer. Much later in life, when he caught his hand in an air-compressor V-belt and broke a finger, though in intense pain, he said simply, "I believe I broke a finger."

W. C. Meloon loved to tinker with all kinds of machinery. He spent much spare time building a boat powered by a Ford Model T engine driving an old airplane propeller. That hobby set in motion the business that was to fluctuate from boom to near bankruptcy and then back to boom again in the ensuing fifty years.

The early years of married life found W. C. and Marion moving rather frequently, trying this and that, anxious to learn what the Lord had in mind for them. After the period of working with his brother in New York, W. C. and his wife moved back to Ossipee where he went into the garage business.

They acquired two garages but both burned down, at different times, one started by a spark from an electric motor igniting gasoline and the other by live ashes being dumped in back of a stable connected to the garage. The Meloons lost materials that required twenty years to repay, and they had no insurance to cover the loss.

Marion had given birth to three sons: Walter Oswald, at Niagara Falls, New York, on October 7, 1915; Ralph C., in Ossipee, New Hampshire, on November 11, 1917, and Harold E., in Providence, Rhode Island, on April 15, 1920. So of course she had her hands full with their care.

But she was always ready to keep books, talk over problems, do banking and related duties. She had completed a brief business course and had a good head for business.

Mother Meloon always held up her end of the work, and perhaps a little more, even lending a hand with the loading on rare occasions.

"Dad," she said one day in her quiet way, "you should have a team of mules instead of a family."

As the children grew old enough to help out at home, Marion put in many long days at the office, working for years without a salary. Eventually, during the World War II contracts, she agreed to accept a modest salary.

W. C. filled the role of family man superbly. With all three sons on his knees during New Hampshire days, he told them stories at bedtime about Buffalo Bill and Wild Bill Hickok, always stopping at the height of suspense with a promise to continue the next night.

When he planned a pheasant hunting trip, his nine-year-old son, Walt, begged to go with him.

"Too cold; too much snow," his dad replied tersely.

When his father arose early next morning, he found Walt waiting in the hall for him, fully dressed. Dad's soft heart yielded to the pleading lad, and the two set out together.

After thirty minutes in the frigid early morning air, Walt's feet began to suffer with the cold. Dad found a farmhouse nearby and left his son with its gracious occupants. Undeterred by the problem he had caused,

O.D.L. campground, Duncan Lake, Ossipee, New Hampshire, featured the first overnight cabins in New England, patterned after cabins at Niagara Falls, New York. This was W. C. Meloon's business enterprise just prior to moving to Florida. It was advertised at the Dover toll bridge to catch northbound traffic by "hand-slingers" which read, "Gas, food, cabins, boats, ponies."

young Walt enjoyed the time of his life with a strange farmer and his wife.

Later, W. C. sold Ford and Dodge cars. When that new venture wore off, the young Meloons became pioneers in a different kind of business, one that today has spread across the nation, though their modest start lasted only briefly and in no way would have seemed to foreshadow such a popular enterprise.

Buying a small piece of property on nearby Duncan Lake, they became forerunners of the flourishing motel industry when, in an effort to improve the property for resale, they built the first tourist cabins the region had ever known. When they sold the property in 1925, they decided to try Florida after persistent urging by two of W. C.'s sisters.

One of the first things Walter noticed about Florida was its many lakes and the contrasting scarcity of boats. It seemed a natural for him to establish the Florida Variety Boat Company with himself as its president. Even the name of the firm allowed plenty of room for experimenting, and that was just what Walter had in mind, though he would be happy to major in boatbuilding if the market warranted.

The Yankee invader constructed his first plant in a central Florida garden spot called Pine Castle, so named by a Florida poet and promoter, William Wallace Harney, who built a castle in the pines in 1870.

In these lovely surroundings, W. C. Meloon struggled with the early birth pangs of his boatbuilding company. His first partner in the new Florida firm, Jephtha Sunday, stayed with the company a year. Seeing no future in the business, he sold his interest. Horace Johnson became Meloon's next partner, and he served in that

27

The Meloons' business began in 1925 under the name,
Florida Variety Boat Company.

capacity for five years before selling out to his col-
league.

Meanwhile, the fast-growing central Florida area
—even in pre-Disney World days—logically would
have gobbled up Pine Castle and made it a part of Orlando. But the tiny town of Edgewood, nestling snugly
in between, almost unnoticed, has prevented the
takeover to this day. The boat company retains an Orlando mailing address primarily because the "City
Beautiful," as Orlando is called, has a substation in Pine
Castle.

Florida Variety Boat Company made no great ripples
in the industry during those early years. In 1930 it
became known as the Pine Castle Boat and Construction
Company. Not until eight years later did the Meloons
begin calling their boats "Correct Craft," and that

W. C. Meloon (*left*) on 1928 trip north with racing hull is shown at Province View Farm in New Hampshire. The sign on the car read, "Boats $35 and up."

popularized label became the name of the company. The firm was incorporated in 1947.

During those transitional years, depression stalked the nation and began to have its effect on the boating industry as well. Three bank failures cost the Meloons all they had, though no large sums figured in the losses.

After the second failure, the company sold a dozen boats to officials at Lake Placid, Florida, a tourist attraction about one-hundred miles south of the plant. When a token down payment proved to be all the buyers would pay after repeated attempts to get the money owed them, the Meloons drove to Lake Placid and collected the $300 still due them. Then they placed it in a bank on Saturday, along with other small checks they had received. The bank closed on Monday.

Mrs. Meloon immediately called all the writers of the checks and asked them to stop payment. They did, and when the original checks were returned to the writers by the bank, they wrote out new checks for the Meloons. Mrs. Meloon's quick thinking thus salvaged something from that disaster.

Employees of the boat company expected to be paid on Saturdays. W. C. often scurried around to sell a rowboat or two, sometimes below cost, to get a few dollars to divide up for salaries. One time he took his wife's last ten dollars to share with his five workers so they could buy groceries. W. C. increased production during one period by nailing a one dollar bill to the wall for each man in the plant.

"When you finish the boat you're working on," he told them, "you can claim your one-dollar bill."

The Reverend O. G. Hall, pastor of the Pine Castle Baptist Church, and W. C. Meloon became close friends. They spent hours talking about spiritual matters and church business. The pastor's wise counsel on one particular subject began to take root in his friend's heart, and W. C. became convinced the Lord would help him pay his bills if he worked only six days a week instead of seven. He set the company policy to prohibit Sunday work. Subsequently, he not only found himself able to pay his own bills, but he also insisted on paying Hall's college debt as well.

The Meloon sons did their best to help out. Ralph, at the age of twelve, began taking company boats and making scenic trips on nearby lakes in 1931 to try to bring in a little something for food and keep the struggling firm afloat.

Walt and two of his cousins, Fred and Bud Jones, helped in the beginning. Later his father's brother,

Uncle Cal, and one of the firm's employees, Frank Ray, joined Ralph, and they began to make longer trips.

The crew traveled from town to town with boats on top of the car or behind, going from one lake to another in search of business. They announced the boat rides by loudspeaker in the town square.

"Only ten and twenty-five cents!" they shouted.

Then they would drive to a nearby lake, launch a boat, and wait for customers.

W. C. paid the men $3 a week. They traveled six to eight weeks at a time, and had hamburger—their only meat—maybe one time during that period. Cal would buy wormy grits and float the worms off. That provided most of their diet. At night they made up their "beds" on garage floors and often saw wharf rats a foot long. Usually they managed to cover up with sheets.

Later, the Meloons put two cars on the road and began to use larger boats, thus attracting larger crowds.

Eventually, Cal Meloon bought the scenic boat business from his brother, W. C., and took it over. Today he lives in Orlando, retired and nearing his eightieth birthday. One incident in particular added a little humor and excitement to the business. It is one of Cal's favorite stories.

A women's garden club took over the whole boat one day on beautiful Lake Osceola. They seemed to be having the time of their lives. Suddenly a mouse ran down the middle of the boat, and Cal quickly sensed the potential danger.

"Ladies!" he shouted. "If you jump out of your seats, you'll turn this boat over!"

Duly warned, the ladies settled down. Suddenly one of the frightened passengers realized that the mouse had run up her dress. She clamped the equally frightened mouse under her arm until the boat was at the dock. Nobody would go after it but Cal, and eventually he retrieved the roving rodent.

Such touches of humor brought lightness and laughter to balance the tears and testings.

4

Harold Finds His Niche

The Meloon sons have experienced an exciting sojourn with faith-inspiring parents. Harold, the youngest, first encountered the boat business in 1927 at the age of seven.

On occasion, he would share portions of the workmen's lunches, sometimes without asking. Eventually, of course, men and management caught on to the youthful pranks and put a halt to Harold's fun. He was reminded of it often for a few days afterward—each time he sat down.

W. C. used to pay his sons a penny a box to pick up bronze screws that happened to get dumped over. Sometimes the boys cheated and dumped the boxes over purposely. But Dad was too smart to let them get by with that kind of thing for long.

Not everything was mischief with the Meloon boys, of course, though to this day Harold's sons call him the family jester. He learned much, of both a humorous and a serious nature, from his father.

As a boy in the church, W. C. Meloon had a future brother-in-law who served as deacon. His kin-to-be always had to have things just right; sometimes this proved a mild frustration for W. C. One Sunday he tied two of the collection baskets together. The ushers picked up the baskets and started out in opposite directions to take the morning offering. Abruptly, they came to a surprised halt.

"My brother-in-law would have killed me if he had known I was responsible," W. C. said.

The senior Meloon loved recreation—sports, hunting, fishing—even though he had little time for extracurricular activities. One day he took all fifteen employees out fishing. "The greatest day of fishing we ever had," Harold described it. The fishermen filled a large, outboard-motor boat full of fish, and they gave part of their prize catch to people all over town.

Occasionally W. C. settled for a shop party at Warren Park. He always seemed to be the life of the party. His love for people, especially children, could not be disguised.

Back in the days when people did not travel much, the three sons and their parents drove up and down the Eastern seaboard on business trips. The boys' knowledge was greatly increased in this way, and their teachers agreed that it was good experience.

The Meloon sons had the privilege, too, of working around equipment and machines, thus putting to good use their natural abilities. When Harold built rowboats in the plant at the age of fourteen, his dad sold them for $16 to $18. He paid his son $2.50 apiece to build them and twenty-five cents each to paint them. Mother Meloon was quite pleased because Harold built two boats a day. That gave him considerable money for a teenager to make in a single day.

One of Harold's part-time jobs bordered on the bizarre. His father made frequent automobile trips, pulling heavy loads of boats and supplies. Harold and his cousin Lyman Hall, now a Baptist preacher in Mascot,

Florida, acted as "brakes" on the trailer. Dad Meloon had rigged a seat right over the axle. The two boys held metal bars, and each of them became responsible for the brake on his side. "Real pioneers in the braking business," they described themselves later.

Today, in his mid-fifties, Harold serves as part-time chaplain and consultant. His expertise as a machinist, tool-and-die maker, welder, and designer makes him a valuable adviser in his hours at the plant. But Harold's heart leans heavily toward his new calling as minister of visitation for Orlando's Sky Lake Baptist Church.

"Lord," he prayed when the surprise call came, "You know I'll be cutting off my source of support."

But he proceeded on faith, and a partial answer came when his mother and two brothers asked him to assume duties as chaplain and consultant at the plant while he performed his new church responsibilities. Serious illnesses and deaths in the boat-firm family bring a personal visit by Harold.

His new church duties began in January 1974 after he had struggled with the decision for several months. The Bible story of Mary and Martha helped him to solve his dilemma.

"Mary hath chosen that good part" (Lk 10:42), and Harold felt he must surely do the same. God had burdened him for a visitation ministry, he knew. That must be His "good part" for the youngest of the three Meloon sons at this crossroads in his career.

The disciples, too, played an integral part in Harold's decision. "Lo, we have left all, and have followed thee" (Mk 10:28). Their example left him no alternative. Solomon added further weight to his pressing call, "Fear God, and keep his commandments; for this is the whole duty of man. For God shall bring every work into judgment, with every secret thing, whether it be good, or whether it be evil" (Ec 12:13-14).

Harold's wife, Jewel, though not physically strong, accompanies him on much of his visitation. They call on unsaved husbands, unsaved wives, hospital patients, and others with personal problems.

"I love to work with my hands," Harold says, "but God made it clear to me He had given me spiritual gifts to be used for His glory. Men and women have thanked me and added, 'You seem to know just what to say,' and that has to be from God."

In his early twenties, as plant engineer, he designed and installed boat trailers, overhead cranes, and boat dollies. This involved him in maintenance, designing of tools, and setting up new divisions.

During World War II, when Correct Craft built pontoon boats for bridges, they had to be handled manually. Harold thought he could come up with a better method. His father had doubts. Buying an old car for $30, Harold and a friend stripped it and built a crane. When W. C. saw the completed device the next day, he walked around it with ill-disguised interest. But he had little to say on the subject.

"What did you do, son, work all night?" he asked. No answer was given, and none was expected.

The crane became a great time and manpower saver, and Correct Craft made much use of the equipment. The company still employs its counterparts today.

In 1945, Harold started his own business, Southern Metal Fabricating Company, near the boat plant in Pine Castle. He built playground equipment for parks and schools, and boat trailers for Correct Craft. Jewel worked with him at the office as much as she could, but she also was busy at home with their four children.

5

Growing Pains

When the Meloons purchased their present two-story, white-stucco office building across the street from the plant, they obtained a super bargain for $600. Even to the present day, the former hotel, sold to them by the bank for unpaid taxes, gives offices downstairs, a home for Mrs. W. C. Meloon upstairs, and an unpaved parking area in the back.

At the outset, it hardly seemed such a bargain, for the roof leaked badly. Oilcloth served as a temporary roof to keep the rain off the beds at night. Sometimes the sound and impact of falling plaster awakened them. At breakfast one morning, an inch-thick avalanche of plaster fell on the table, barely missing the diners as they ate.

In spite of those early drawbacks, the Meloon home felt the warmth of many happy family gatherings on holidays and anniversaries. W. C. piled children and, later, grandchildren, on his back, then galloped around the room on all fours while the children squealed with delight. He frequently challenged family members to Indian wrestle with him. Grandfather beat them all, until the later years of his life.

Anxious to see every loved one possess faith in Jesus Christ, W. C. looked for ways to share a natural witness.

When he took a trip to South Carolina to pick up some fiberglass materials, he invited a grandson, Ralph, Jr., to accompany him. Then, in a careful and tactful way, he spent much of the travel time discussing the lad's lifestyle. Similarly, he exercised his strong spiritual influence over all his progeny.

A photographer for the *Orlando Sentinel-Star* newspaper, who was assigned to take pictures at the Titusville plant several times, had lunch or dinner with W. C. Meloon on occasion. "Your dad taught me to give thanks at the table," he told Harold one day.

World War II brought a sudden upsurge in boatbuilding, so the Meloons began to seek a logical site for a second plant. Titusville, some fifty miles east of Pine Castle on the Atlantic Coast and just a short distance from famed Cape Canaveral, seemed a natural place.

The Correct Craft plant in Titusville, Florida, operated from 1942 to 1955. It is no longer standing.

Convinced that the addition of a Correct Craft plant in the town would enhance its economy, Titusville officials gave property to the Meloons on a sixty-year lease. Donors and recipients had not reckoned on the opposition of World War II veterans, however. These young men learned that the property had been dedicated as a park, and that an act of the legislature should be required to sell it.

Walt Meloon appeared at a special city council hearing called to reconsider the gift. He discussed a multimillion-dollar contract Correct Craft might receive and what it would do for the city. His appearance, however, only seemed to stir up the opposition. Some wanted to break the lease and evict the Meloons from the city. Heightening Walt's concern was the fact that the company needed to increase its net worth so it could obtain a bond issue to cover the bond required by the government before they would give the contract for the nineteen-foot boats Correct Craft built in 1951 for the Korean War. A number of contracts were involved, and the Meloons finally received them all—a total of 400 boats.

Young men of the opposition sought support up and down the streets. Feeling became so negative that Ann Meloon feared to make the trip to the grocery store. The pressure began to change the council members' feelings about their gift of property to the boatbuilders. The case against the Meloons seemed hopeless. Then Walt encountered a friend, Dewey Fisk, who suggested a maneuver he had seen work successfully in a similar situation.

"I know a fellow who paid his entire payroll one time in silver dollars," Fisk said. "That way he knew where the money was being spent. If you will do the same, the

Nineteen-foot bridge-erection boats, M3 assault boats, and pontoon-bridge boats was built for the U.S. Army by the Meloons during World War II and the Korean War.

business people in this city will know where their money is coming from."

Walt Meloon had no other ideas to stem the tide. He began to consider the possibility of such a strange move.

"The silver dollars will have to come from the Federal Reserve Bank in Atlanta," he was told.

A few days later, bank officials delivered a wheelbarrow full of silver dollars to the Meloons. They placed the money in bags, with names of the employees on them.

About thirty minutes after distribution of the payroll, the A. & P. grocery store manager called the Meloons.

"Walt, don't pull that trick again," he pleaded. "I can't close my cash drawer!"

Other stores had similar problems. Headlines the next morning read: "Correct Craft Pays Payroll in Silver Dollars; Chokes Cash Registers."

The point had been made. A week later, the Meloons offered the city $1 for the property. City council members called a special meeting to act on the offer.

"I move that we keep Correct Craft and let them have the property so they can get this contract," a councilman began. One of his colleagues seconded the motion, and the council passed it unanimously without debate.

In subsequent days, bankers from several towns and cities came to Titusville and offered loans to the Meloons so they could build the planned warehouse.

Ray Carroll, president of the First National Bank of Kissimmee, in cooperation with ten other banks, arranged to lend W. C. Meloon $500,000. A few days later, Carroll—in deep distress—came to the boat executive.

"Mr. Meloon," he said, "I'm in terrible shape. The bank examiner has just come and declared the loan illegal. He is going to close all our banks. We would have to have mortgages on property to cover all this."

At that strategic moment, a representative of the city of Titusville delivered the property deed to the Meloons.

"Ray," W. C. asked, "would this be enough to get the examiners off our backs?"

That did prove to be the lifesaving move, and the Kissimmee Bank has loaned money to Correct Craft for many years.

W. C. Meloon seized the opportunity to share spiritual truths he had been learning with his wife and family—prophetic words they would not soon forget.

"God's going to continue guiding us," he began. "There will be serious problems, perhaps even in the family and among our members, but He will bless us as He has in the past.

"God has had to punish us at times, even as He did the

41

children of Israel. During the hard times, I've lived with Daniel, with Moses, with Job. How in the world could we come up with more than we ever had before? God did it for us."

Meanwhile, an editorial in the Titusville newspaper, helped to bolster the Correct Craft relationship with the city. "Estimating four to a family," the editorial read, "the total number of people living off the Correct Craft payroll is 1,040, which is about a third or fourth of our population. This does not take into consideration the indirect benefits of a plant like that in a community."

Walt Meloon became general manager of the Titusville plant, which soon had 300 employees on its rolls. Correct Craft remained in the East Coast city from 1942 to 1955. The Titusville plant was sold in 1960, and later was leveled to the ground.

A sound philosophy of Christian living and witness, born in the crucible of experience, has characterized the lives of Meloon family members.

6

Heart of a Man

Union men began to try to organize at both Correct Craft plants in 1951. Max K. Aulick, now in public relations for the boatbuilders, had his own problems with the union negotiators at the time.

From 1934 to 1971, Aulick operated both the Southern Lighting Manufacturing Company and the Orlando Boat Company. His firms made gas tanks for Correct Craft boats and helped to manufacture some components for the first military aluminum bridge-erection boats, also built by the Meloons.

During his meetings with the union men, Aulick noticed that they suddenly discontinued their efforts to organize Correct Craft.

"How did it happen that you dropped Correct Craft?" he asked.

"Do you want to know the truth?" responded the union negotiator.

"Yes," Aulick said.

"Every time we went over there and started a meeting to discuss negotiations, W. C. Meloon insisted on praying before the discussion began. The union organizer got so tired of the praying he decided to forget the whole thing."

That same dependence on divine aid carried over into every area of Walt Meloon's life as well. Anxious to share his faith with his employees as an extension of his Sunday worship, he conducted his first plant chapel service at the Titusville location in 1943. Jimmy Sutherland, now president of the Baptist Bible Institute in Graceville, Florida, spoke at the first service. Eight years later, Billy Graham attracted the largest chapel attendance at Correct Craft when 1,000 visitors helped to make the crowd overflow the plant. Many people responded to the invitation to receive Christ as Saviour that day.

Later, Grady Wilson and four other Billy Graham team members—Cliff Barrows, Beverly Shea, Paul Mikkelsen, and Tedd Smith—held a week of services in both plants. A seventy-six-year-old rancher-oilman-cowboy, Sam Meanes, from West Texas, an admirer of the Meloon family, spent his entire honeymoon week with his new bride at the Pine Castle plant services. Many decisions resulted from the dual meetings.

Pioneers in industrial evangelism, the Meloons have continued chapel services down through the years, though now they are held twice monthly instead of weekly. Longer presentations, such as the Billy Graham films, brought about the change.

Many lives have been favorably affected for eternity because of these special plant meetings. Employees are not required to attend the chapel service, but most do take advantage of the inspirational hour. They know they will not be embarrassed in any way and more than likely will be challenged and helped. Some seek further counsel; others resist. Ralph Meloon experienced great joy in leading a Correct Craft truck driver, John Bishop, to Christ after praying for him for twenty years.

One long-time employee credited W. C. Meloon's consistent life, more than the chapel services, with making the deepest impression on him.

"He was as close to me as any man could ever be outside of my own dad," truck driver Slim Guthrie said. "I worked with him day in and day out. He never asked an employee to do anything that he wouldn't do himself. He always had time to say a cheery word to you no matter where you were. When he was intent on business, nothing else mattered—his clothes or his own well-being.

"One cold December day we were putting in a boat dock on a lake. He drove the car right down to the edge of the water. He walked out into the water in his good clothes—up to his waist—showing me where the dock should go.

"When he came out of the water he warned me, 'I've got to stay out of Mother's sight until my clothes dry or she'll kill me.'

"One time we were testing a boat that a dealer had said was faulty. 'Slim,' Mr. Meloon said to me, 'we're going to prove this dealer is wrong.' He was driving, and we opened the boat wide. The steering mechanism came loose and he had no control of it. The boat zigzagged so much he couldn't reach the key to turn the motor off. Finally he managed to reach it and stop the boat.

"'Slim,' he said to me with a wry smile, 'I guess that's one time the dealer was right. Can you fix the steering mechanism so we can ease this boat back to the dock?'

"I was able to do this after tinkering with it awhile. Believe me, we crawled back to that dock.

"He had a real faith at any time of the day or night. His

45

life could fill several books, and nothing bad would be in any of them."

Dad Meloon possessed a calmness and serenity that surprised and sometimes frustrated his friends. He refused to acknowledge anyone as his enemy. When a man with a real or imagined grievance avoided him on the sidewalk one day as they passed, Meloon walked briskly around the block. He confronted his "enemy" again and engaged him in friendly conversation. Competitors and creditors found it impossible to remain angry with him.

One personal hobby consumed the boat executive's interest during a prosperous period. He bought and bred beautiful horses—up to thirty-one at a time—one of them a five-gaited saddle horse. Not until prices on horses hit bottom and he could not afford to feed and breed them any longer did W. C. discontinue his hobby. He gave several of the animals to Hampden-DuBose Academy, a Christian school in nearby Zellwood, to use as their saddle horses.

But hobbies never occupied more than a small amount of his time. Even his competitors considered him a top designer and promoter who was "way ahead of his time." They knew he did not hesitate to venture out into new fields of boat design. He summed up his philosophy of work in a couplet: "If we are to give our employer his best, we must get our night's rest." When the clock struck 9 P.M. he would excuse himself and go to bed.

Until the day he died, W. C. Meloon spent time on his knees beside his bed each evening. When burdens troubled him during the night, he arose and prayed until the Lord satisfied him that everything was all right.

Once Dad Meloon served on a committee to put a new

roof on the church. When a friend on the committee recommended a new kind of metal roofing, the senior Meloon took his word for it. Unfortunately, the roof leaked like a sieve.

"How much did it cost?" W. C. asked.

After learning the amount, he wrote out a check and gave it to the church. He assumed full blame for the defective material.

W. C. instilled in his sons a deep sense of reverence and respect for womanhood, influenced no doubt by six fine sisters and a wife of highest character. That respect for the Meloon women evidences itself today throughout the family. Only God Himself claimed and received more respect from the senior Meloon.

7

A Philadelphian Comes to the Plant

In spite of all that his parents could say or do, the oldest son, Walt, like many youths, lost interest in school in his mid-teens, so he was put to work in the plant. Jack Dunn of Old Forge, New York came down to Daytona Beach one winter and noticed Walt's capable handling of boats. He invited the seventeen-year-old to come to work with him as a Chris-Craft distributor, first in Old Forge and later in Daytona. Dad Meloon gave his approval, despite a dissenting vote from his wife, and Walt left home for three years to undertake the excitement and adventure of a new position and a new location.

After two years with Chris-Craft, his wanderlust took him to Palm Beach, Florida, where he worked for the Sea Bantam Company. Meanwhile, he "graduated" from the drugstore soda fountain to beer joints and picked up a prized tobacco pipe along the way. Walt had been in Palm Beach about a year when he received a wire from his parents urging him to come home and take a job that was open.

Grasping the wire in one hand, Walt went out to the boatyard. "See here," he said to his co-workers. "They finally have discovered they can't do without me at home."

With that kind of attitude, plus a pipe in his mouth, Walt walked into his mother's kitchen a few days later. As he entered, she walked out. Walt's grandmother, also in the room, stood her ground.

"Walter," she began, "don't you ever do that again. You have broken your mother's heart." Walt went back to work for the family firm, now convinced the other pasture is not always greener.

Some years later, in 1945, while representing Correct Craft at a boat show in Philadelphia, Walt met Norman M. Sewell. The highly successful businessman had accepted a friend's invitation to look at the first plywood Correct Craft boat. Walt and Sewell liked what they saw in each other and had a wonderful time talking about the Lord and boats, which provided a hobby and relaxation for Sewell.

The Pennsylvania executive had a sixty-acre farm in the Philadelphia area, maintained a business, and served as vice-president of ten organizations. Four years after meeting Walt Meloon, Norm Sewell was sidelined for awhile with physical problems that culminated in nervous fatigue. His doctor told him he must get away from the pressures causing his exhausted condition. He took his family to Florida, and after trying various things he asked the Meloons for a job in 1951.

Almost from the start of his employment with Correct Craft, Sewell urged consideration of a house organ for the company. He finally convinced the Meloons that the idea was a good one; and he became the organizer, founder, and first editor of the Orlando Tribune. In 1958 he became export manager of Correct Craft, then sales manager in 1964 before his retirement in 1970.

Norm, as his many friends call him, made a significant contribution to the firm, boosting its export business to nearly 8 percent of its total production. Somewhere between 4 and 5 percent is considered good.

Despite his retirement, Sewell is teaching a course in exporting at Mid-Florida Tech and writing a primer textbook on the subject. His years of experience at Correct Craft led to his appointment by Secretary of Commerce Maurice H. Stans as a member of the National Export Expansion Council and chairman of the Regional Export Expansion Council.

Sewell recalls how Mrs. W. C. Meloon used to call him every two or three weeks.

"Mr. Sewell," she said, "will you please take a trip out to the plant and pick up Dad's shirts?"

Norm found as many as nine shirts at one time, scattered around in various places where W. C. had removed them to perform some task. Several ties usually could be found nearby.

Another time, Mrs. Meloon called Norm to alert him.

"Will you watch out for some bankers who are coming to the plant today? We're anxious to make a good impression so that we can get a loan. Be sure to see that Dad is properly dressed when they come."

When the bankers arrived, they began to ask questions about Mr. Meloon. Sewell thought it best to pave the way for whatever they might find.

"If you see someone with his sleeves rolled up," he suggested, "probably that will be Mr. Meloon."

But what they did not expect to see was a grease-covered man lifting up a boat. Fortunately, what they saw impressed the bankers. Not every firm had its president pitching in to do even the dirtiest work.

Norm Sewell proved to be just the man Correct Craft

and the Meloons needed overseas. With dignity and decorum, tact and diplomacy, he represented the boat-builders at international trade fairs in many countries. His wife, Ellen, added grace to such occasions, and their cordial goodwill paid off in export sales and many other ways.

Though Correct Craft, Inc., is largely a Meloon operation, Norm Sewell is typical of many others who have played a vital part in its success.

George Beverly Shea sang at a New York boat show breakfast sponsored by Correct Craft. Walter O. Meloon is at the left, and Norman Sewell at the right.

8

On the Edge of Bankruptcy

World War II came to a sudden end in 1945, and Walt Meloon left his Titusville home to begin traveling coast to coast and even into Canada and Cuba in sales, heralding the Correct Craft name. While the boatbuilders designed new and bigger boats, up to fifty-footers selling for $86,000, Walt continued to hit the highways, selling more of the company's products and signing up new dealers.

In 1960, when decreased production led to sale of the Titusville plant, the Meloons quit building the bigger boats. Today's models measure no more than twenty-four feet.

Boat sales fluctuated precariously, but the Meloons managed to stay on an even keel spiritually. When the Christian Business Men's Committee of Orlando had organized in 1943, Walt had become a charter member. His father and two brothers attended many of the new group's functions, but were not active members, primarily because of already full schedules. Ralph and Walt also worked with the Gideons in their program of Bible distribution.

While in Titusville, Walt had served as a deacon in the First Baptist Church. Ralph has been a deacon in Pine Castle's First Baptist Church, where all three brothers responded to the Gospel invitation at the same time in 1927. Shortly after their conversion, they entered the waters of baptism together.

Between boatbuilding and work for the Lord, the Meloons had little time for civic or social efforts. But the time came when business leaders in Titusville asked Walt if he would consider serving as the Titusville Chamber of Commerce president.

"After the first meeting," Walt responded with mock seriousness, "you wouldn't have me."

"Why?" they asked.

"If I were president," Walt replied, "the chamber of commerce wouldn't have any cocktail parties or dances. Every meeting would begin with prayer offered by a pastor or a layman who has a good Christian testimony in the community."

Chamber officials considered Walt's conditions for several days. Then they came back and asked him to serve as their president on his own terms. Walt filled the position capably for two terms, marked by a conspicuous absence of cocktail parties and dances. His associate, Dick Parks, the chamber's paid secretary, accompanied Walt when he spoke in churches on Sundays and served as his song leader.

Correct Craft began sliding toward bankruptcy in 1957. The company had experienced an earlier climb with a government contract for 3,000 boats, one of many such agreements the firm had enjoyed since before the war.

Now the chief of the three-man inspection team sat across the table from Walt and Ralph Meloon as they sought to iron out details of the contract. He eyed the papers carefully.

"Did you know," the chief inspector asked, "that

you're one of only two companies in the whole south-east that do not have someone on their payroll who carries an expense account to take care of the inspectors' expenses?" His smile seemed rather grim.

"No, I didn't," Walt said, feeling his way carefully, yet knowing that the government actually took care of such expenses. The inspector's sullen look brought a sense of uneasiness to the Correct Craft official.

Two weeks later, when sixteen-foot fiber-glass boats began coming down the production line, Ralph approached Walt with concern clearly etched on his face. "Those government people are rejecting an awful lot of boats," he said.

"Well," Walt countered, "we don't want to deliver anything that isn't right."

"True," Ralph said, "but tiny blemishes are clearly allowable under terms of the contract."

When the high rate of rejections continued, the Meloons decided on an experiment. They took one of the rejected boats, cleaned off the inspector's chalk marks, and sent it back through the line on a later shift. This time it passed.

The silent war continued. At times the Meloons thought, *Why not pay the man off? It really isn't much compared to what the company stands to lose.*

"It wasn't the money," Walt said, "but something far deeper. At night I'd lie awake wrestling with the problem. Trying not to disturb my wife, Ann, I would slip out of bed, go to the living room, and kneel on the floor, my open Bible on a stool before me."

(Ann always knew when Walt slipped out of bed to pray, and she would be praying too in bed.)

"I would pray and talk with the Lord," Walt continued, "and He would lead me through His Word. In the light of my living room lamp one night, these words seemed to glow: 'Trust in the LORD with all thine heart; and lean not unto thine own understanding. In all thy ways acknowledge him, and he shall direct thy paths.'

"That had to be our answer," Walt added. "To pay off the man would not be trusting the Lord but, rather, giving in to the devious ways of the world."

The Meloons tried many avenues of relief and found nothing but closed doors. Rejected boats piled up in the storage yard. Reading the Bible one night, Walt wondered if the Lord had forgotten them. He expressed his concern in prayer. An inner voice responded: "Have you forgotten the storm boats and what I did for you then?" Perhaps he had lost sight too soon of the miracle production.

Now, with that clear reminder from the Lord, the Meloons took heart and moved ahead. They would do what they could, short of dishonesty, to satisfy the government. By year's end they had delivered 2,200 boats, and 600 rejects remained in the storage yard. Then came the final blow.

A flatcar had just been loaded with forty "approved" boats. The chief inspector suddenly appeared just as the switch engine backed up to the flatcar. He turned to Walt Meloon.

"I don't like their looks," he said, pointing to the boats. "They've got to be unloaded and refinished."

That arbitrary decision, unfair as it was, made it impossible to continue. The contract already had cost the company one million dollars, and Correct Craft now owed $500,000 to 228 creditors. Also, the bank had withdrawn all its commitments.

At a specially called meeting, the creditors heard the full story. The Meloons promised to pay them as soon as possible and asked for suggestions. One creditor recommended that the firm seek protection under chapter 11 of the Bankruptcy Act, which allows management to continue in the interest of creditors. Others agreed to that implicit vote of confidence in the Meloon integrity, and in August 1958 that step was taken. But how they would build boats without money was a question that deeply disturbed the Meloons.

"I'll never forget that night when I walked into our silent plant," Walt recalled. "The floor that once hummed with busy workers was now deserted. I knew how Joseph must have felt as he was dragged down that long dusty road to Egypt. We had done everything man could do. Now it was in the Lord's hands."

9

The Struggle Upward

Meanwhile, *things worsened at the plant, and in a* joint effort to ease the situation, every employee resigned. The Meloons "rehired" those employees considered absolutely essential to the operation. Ralph's wife, Betty, worked the switchboard for awhile, but it was not an easy job.

Then Ann took over. She was not very eager for the task, but Walt felt that many of the creditors and dealers had met her personally or had been entertained in the Meloon home. They would recognize her voice and like the idea that the president's wife responded to their calls.

Sometimes she was able to answer questions or clear up misunderstandings without disturbing Walt. Other times she was able to find out the nature of the call and alert Walt so that he could take a moment to pray for wisdom before answering the call.

Walt returned a newly purchased Lincoln car to the dealer and drove the old company pickup for awhile. Often the Meloons walked instead of driving, to demonstrate their willingness to adjust to the economic stress.

The senior Meloons never went to court during all the bankruptcy proceedings. Their sons chose to spare them the ordeal. But they, too, faced harassment day after day from anxious creditors and the referee in bankruptcy, and they, too, experienced sleepless nights of waiting upon God for a solution.

"Our first answer," Walt said, with characteristic candor, "was a gift of enough guts to get up and face the situation each day. And that was no small victory. God didn't give us comfort at that time, but He did give faith enough to face the next morning."

The Meloons had found that their assets were just about even with their liabilities, but it did not look as if this could continue. The trend seemed heavily in the wrong direction. God answered this dilemma with a series of "miracles" that temporarily eased the burden.

First came a loan from a business friend in Norway, Torry Mosvold of the Mosvold Shipping Company in

Cliff Barrows, song leader for evangelist Billy Graham, spoke at a 1956 boat show breakfast in New York City sponsored by Correct Craft. Walt Meloon is fifth from left; W. C. Meloon, third from left.

58

At a Chicago boat show breakfast sponsored by Correct Craft, Walt Meloon, president, and his wife Ann, are seated at the center of the speaker's table. Also seated at the table are W. C. Meloon (*fifth from right*), speaker Waldo Yeager of CBMC of Toledo (*sixth from right*), Don Hustad (*far left*), George Beverly Shea (*second from left*), Ted Engstrom (*third from left*), and Ralph C. Meloon (*fifth, next to Ann*).

Kristiansand, to tide them over. The Meloons had met the Scandinavian magnate through a mutual friend, Gus Gustafson, who had left New York in the mid-'50s to become controller of Correct Craft. For many years the Meloons had sponsored a breakfast for their boat friends as a part of the boat shows in New York and Chicago. Mosvold had come as a guest of Gustafson to hear Jack Wyrtzen address the crowd.

Then came a letter from Pakistan, written on paper that looked like newsprint. It had misspellings and crossed out words. The writer, retired Pakistani Army Major Moodi Farouki, asked for a quotation on boats like those the Meloons had built in 1951 for the U.S. Army. Evidently the U.S. government had given some of the boats to Pakistan.

59

The Meloons, not anxious to add more problems to the growing turmoil, filed the letter away—unanswered. Why go halfway around the world to seek a partial solution to their dilemma? They reasoned that they had enough problems close to home.

Several weeks later, another letter came from Farouki.

"Would you please do me the courtesy of answering my previous correspondence?" he pleaded.

This time, a reply went forward immediately. That began a flurry of correspondence that culminated in a $139,000 contract from the government of Pakistan. One of the rejected sixteen-foot plastic boats was shipped to the minister of defense in Pakistan, with the notice that many others were available. An order came back for 239 of the rejected boats.

Several days later a phone call came to the Meloons at about 3 A.M. It was from Pakistan.

"Hello," a voice said indistinctly, "I'm Moodi Farouki. We've been corresponding. What kind of people are you?"

"What do you mean, what kind of people are we?" Walt Meloon asked, unsure of the question's intent.

"The U.S. government has sent a man over here to tell our minister of defense that you people are not honorable, and not to do business with you."

Walt thought a moment before replying.

"Well, Moodi," he said, "I can't answer all your questions by phone, but I'll be glad to correspond further with you. What is this going to mean?"

Farouki responded, without hesitation.

"My government is cancelling those two contracts."

The harried Meloons reacted initially with understandable shock. Their friends in Norway had sent an additional $40,000 loan, and that had already been spent. Now the contracts were being canceled. Where would they turn next? True, God had seen them through difficult situations before, but maybe this was too much for Him. Their hearts knew better, but their heads kept trying to get in the way.

Somehow, after the initial shock, the Meloons regained their confidence and composure. They had asked the Lord not to allow them to have the contracts from Pakistan unless it was truly His will. A cable the following morning confirmed the cancellation. The comptroller and treasurer insisted on halting production on the boats immediately. But the Meloons remained firm. The Lord had led; they would not lose faith now.

Meanwhile, the first large boat and ten smaller boats already had been shipped to Pakistan. Ten days later, a check came for the eleven boats. The Meloons decided to send a few more to see what would happen. A check came back! Correct Craft kept sending the small boats until all 239 of them had been shipped and paid for by the Pakistan Embassy. The Meloons' faith again had been rewarded.

"The story of Moses' forty years in the wilderness didn't mean a thing to me," Walt Meloon said, "until we spent six years going through the same kinds of experiences. I had to sit with Job in the ashes and say, 'Why me, Lord?' Job never did turn against God. He said, 'Though he slay me, yet will I trust in him,' and I went to bed many a night with those words on my lips.

"I learned much from these experiences," Walt continued. "All through these trying times, I was awakened by early-morning phone calls—usually from our creditors. Not able to get back to sleep, I would go to the living room, get down the Bible, and read. Then I spent much time in prayer.

"I talked with the Lord about the problems—mostly about myself—and then looked to Him for the answers. Many days I prayed, 'Lord, if You'll keep the sheriff from putting a lock on the door, I'll go back and work until the time comes when You see fit to deliver us from the problem.'"

This by no means solved all the financial problems. "But by now," Walt said, "we had learned to really relax and trust God. A few years previously I would have found it difficult to spend fifteen minutes at a time in prayer. Now I was spending up to an hour or more each day on my knees. And we continued working, and paying our creditors."

In times like this, the Meloons discovered, you learn who are your real friends, and you lose a few fair-weather friends.

Bud Coleman, owner of a local automobile agency, had loaned money to W. C. Meloon on mortgages on the plant property. For about ten years, the boatbuilders lacked funds to pay even the interest. Whenever they visited with Coleman or he called on the phone, it was to ask for parts for a boat and to ask about the senior Meloons and other members of the family.

Never once did he say, "When are you going to start paying?" Or, "I'm going to have to turn this over to an attorney."

The Meloons never felt uncomfortable in his presence. Finally, the day came when they could go to him and ask what his books showed they owed.

Coleman produced a report showing the condition of the account. He had not compounded the interest for the ten years but had added only each yearly amount of interest and then totaled it with the principal. The Meloons' amazement turned to gratitude to God.

An official of Bailey Motors and Equipment Company called the firm almost immediately after it had to file under chapter 11.

"We know you have had some troubles," he said, "and you probably still have some troubles, but we are confident you will come out of it all right. We want you to feel free to come down any time and get what you need."

That phone call came in the midst of a strenuous and pressing afternoon. It was like a cool waterfall to the troubled Meloon family. Others proved not so patient, and their short memories in later years amused the boatbuilders.

On occasion, one of the Meloons will meet a former creditor on the street. "That bankruptcy was some rough time for all of us, wasn't it?" begins the time-of-day comment. "We were glad to help you through it."

The Meloon family spent many times together at midnight and after, drawn by a common desire and sense of need to pray. Pressure seemed to galvanize them into a well-knit unit. Earlier tensions vanished in the white heat of spiritual warfare.

"I'll do anything to help" became the Meloon battle cry. Family members shared favorite scripture verses, by which their hearts had been newly quickened. God gave great comfort and peace to each of them as they faced misunderstanding and harassment.

Today, when someone with bankruptcy problems talks to Walt Meloon about his difficulty, the boatbuilder asks him, "What is it you really want to solve? If the Holy Spirit does what He really wants to do in your situation, He will make it a testimony, a blessing, to you and to others. He won't necessarily release you from it."

Walt adds: "As Christians, sometimes we have a tendency to quit when things go wrong. I don't believe this is pleasing to the Lord. Proverbs says we shouldn't despise the chastening of the Lord; it brings 'sweet results' in the end."

An enlightenment, as the Meloons called it, occurred next in the line of miracles. It led company officials to set up five factory warehouse distribution centers in scattered areas of the United States. Family members operated most of them. These autonomous centers, first of their kind in the boating industry, proved successful in selling Correct Craft boats to dealers in their areas, tapping new markets, and generating new income.

"In effect," Walt explained, "these five satellite companies acted as flotation barges around a sunken ship, lifting us to the surface. As a result, Correct Craft again became healthy and growing."

Through all of the hard places, God raised up friends—His messengers—to supply comfort, encouragement, and material help when needed most. Walt knew that he and the rest of the family would never cease to marvel at the number of God's servants who had been used to influence their lives. One in particular—a blind man—stood out. His name was Albert B. Johnson, and he helped to make the difficult days bearable.

10

Blind Samaritan

Harried, pressured Meloons needed friends during the days of bankruptcy proceedings more than ever before. Not only did they need a heavenly Friend who "sticketh closer than a brother" but also earthly friends who might provide solace, comfort, counsel. They found many, but one in particular was outstanding.

A. B. Johnson, founder of Orlando's best known electrical firm and a blind man with unusual abilities, had known the boatbuilding family through activities of the Christian Business Men's Committee of Orlando, an evangelistically minded group of laymen who carried their Christian witness over into weekdays as they pursued their business and professional careers.

An occasional golf game together—with the sightless Johnson often shooting in the 80s—brought the men closer together. Walt Meloon, in particular, spent some time on the links with the electric executive. Inevitably, some of the boatbuilding problems came to light. Johnson had suffered through financial straits in earlier years, and now he wanted to help his friends by sharing his invaluable bankruptcy experience.

When he learned that the Correct Craft firm planned to add a badly needed warehouse valued at some $40,000 on its Pine Castle property, Johnson entered a

Helping Great-Granddad W. C. Meloon at the ground-breaking ceremony for the new building are (*left to right*) Craig and Jeff Warner, and Lori and Gary Meloon.

bid from the Johnson Electric Company to do the wiring. Deliberately bidding low to make sure his plan would work, Johnson got the job for his firm.

Now entitled to attend the creditors' meetings, often when none of the Meloons had been invited, A. B.—as he was affectionately known by scores of central Floridians—"scouted" the meetings for his friends. His wise counsel over a period of many weeks and months kept the Meloon family from being forced out of management of the firm.

Johnson often would call his friend on a Tuesday or Friday evening. "Walt," he would say, "this is the boss speaking. I expect to see you out on the golf course tomorrow morning."

The friendly prodding paid dividends in many ways. Meloon not only kept his sanity in the midst of an "impossible" situation, but he also received words of wisdom on how to proceed in the future.

"I came to love that man about as much as anyone on earth," Walt said. "To know him as a friend was one of the greatest experiences of my life."

When A. B. Johnson died, his oldest son, Bob, called Walt early in the morning. "Dad got his eyesight back today," he said.

To the present day, Walt often recounts his warm association with Johnson, an important by-product of his bankruptcy trials. Occasionally Walt and Bob play golf together today, and an unusual drive or putt brings a poignant comment from the boatbuilder. "I wonder what A. B. thought of that shot," he says.

Ralph Godwin, an Orlando pastor at the time, made a startling observation to Walt one day. "You know," he

W. C. Meloon (*center*) awaits other visitors for the dedication of the new building in Pine Castle.

67

said, "A. B. took on the likeness of the Holy Spirit in one very real way. By purposely becoming a creditor, he got into the problem with you to try to help you work it out. He loved you that much."

Walt feels, too, that he learned much from the wit and wisdom of his blind friend. Some months before his passing, while golfing with a nephew, A. B. Johnson and his young relative suddenly found themselves confronted with a gigantic thunderstorm. Jagged streaks of lightning pierced the skies. A. B. laughed as they scurried to a nearby tree.

"Surely," he said, "the lightning won't find us under there."

Only moments later, a blinding flash struck the tree and slammed the two men to the ground. Both fell unconscious, but soon thanked God together as they regained consciousness.

Several years after A. B.'s death, a tornado struck and completely uprooted the very same tree under which the two men had sought refuge on the golf course. Walt Meloon read the news with interest.

"Well," he said to Bob Johnson, "it took your dad quite a while to get around to it, but he finally got rid of that tree!"

Such was the comaraderie between two men who sought to please the Lord in every area of their lives, and to demonstrate quietly and unostentatiously the love of Christ toward each other. To this day, the Meloons consider A. B. Johnson one of the Lord's prime instruments in bringing them successfully through the bankruptcy battles.

With that kind of spiritual assistance, the Meloons found their way eased considerably as they struggled through the bankruptcy proceedings. When the attorney for the creditors called for a hearing in Tampa to have the Meloon family removed from the company's management, A. B. Johnson insisted on riding from Orlando in the car with the Meloons rather than with other members of the creditors' committee.

Attorney Jim Welch, company controller Ray White, and Johnson accompanied the Meloons.

"Lord," they prayed as they traveled, "we know the charges are largely true. We have made mistakes. We need about forty-five days to get the problems straightened out."

The Orlando contingent arrived in Tampa only moments before the hearing proceeded in the federal court building. Soon it seemed the time had come for the referee to agree with the creditors' attorney. That would put the Meloons out of management, with the company in the hands of a receiver. At this critical juncture, the attorney for the creditors felt he had an important point to contribute to the hearing.

"The Meloons distributed $10,000 among their creditors," he complained, "and didn't even tell me anything about it."

The referee listened, then stiffened noticeably as his face flushed. He had been the one who signed the checks in question!

"It isn't necessary for you to be told what was done," he responded rather gruffly. "The court gave the order to do this."

Then he took his gavel and pounded on the desk.

"I'll be prepared to hear more on the Correct Craft matter on March 15 in Orlando," he said.

In the car going home, one of the men suddenly thought to count the number of days before the next hearing. There were not the forty-five days they had prayed for, but forty-six!

When the time arrived for the hearing in Orlando, the Meloons still had not found a solution to their financial problems. The opening move by the creditors' attorney caught them completely by surprise.

"Judge," he said to the referee, "I don't know why, but since the hearing in Tampa my clients have asked that I withdraw the complaints."

In three minutes, the hearing concluded. An important skirmish had been won.

Finally, after six years of negotiations, the referee retired and the court appointed another referee. He notified Correct Craft and the creditors that he was going to liquidate the company in ten days. The small creditors had been paid off, and 101 of them received 100 percent of what Correct Craft owed them.

A letter to the remaining 127 creditors asked a pertinent question.

"Would you accept a settlement of 10 percent from the Meloon family within six months, in lieu of the judge putting us out of business?"

All but one creditor agreed to the settlement; and when the referee's subsequent contact with the creditors confirmed the earlier findings, he released the Meloons from chapter 11 of the Bankruptcy Act on the first business day of 1965.

Instead of a 10 percent settlement with the large creditors, the Meloons actually made a 5 percent payment, followed shortly thereafter by a 10 percent and then another 5 percent payment.

"We learned," Walt said, "there is no such thing as having a greater need than the ability of God to take care of that need. We wouldn't have missed this experience for a million dollars, but I wouldn't give fifteen cents for another one just like it!''

Perhaps the last thing in the world the Meloons wanted or expected was an invitation to share the whole sordid story of bankruptcy. But that assignment came to them, and still does—not once, but often. The humbling experience continues to reap eternal dividends.

11

Adventure on the Alcan

God did not answer prayer only when they worked hard, the Meloons discovered. He was as much their God on recreational trips as in business ventures and personal problems.

In 1959, financial pressures became almost too heavy to bear. Ralph Meloon, then president and the only son continuously with Correct Craft from the beginning, heeded the advice of his family and friends and set out for the newly proclaimed state of Alaska with his wife, Betty, and two sons, Ken and Ralph, Jr. Daughter Marian had been recently married. The trip would include some business, as Ralph wanted to find possible dealer locations and see how the boating industry fared in other parts of the country.

The harried executive and his family traveled the long, hard route to the frozen northland, never sure they were going to be able to continue, and not certain if they even wanted to complete the journey. They drove through Memphis, Tennessee; Lincoln, Nebraska; and Oneida, South Dakota, where Dad Meloon had been born; then on through Minot, North Dakota, to Canada, camping in a tent along the way.

They lacked the money to room elsewhere, but they

would not if they could, since camping was a favorite family pastime whenever they could get away. Ralph, Jr., particularly loved to camp way back in the woods away from the road, in hopes he would see some wild animals. His mother bravely went along with his desire for backwoods spots, meanwhile praying they *would* *not* see any large, wild animals.

They entered the Alcan Highway by way of Dawson Creek, British Columbia, and reached the Peace River. One of the bridges had been destroyed earlier by storms. Only a railroad bridge remained. Placing boards on the rails, their car followed others 100 feet apart as they made the perilous crossing. The tense travelers looked into the valley 200 feet below as the car crept across. God again kept His hand on them.

The Alcan proved to be a tremendous challenge. With no paved roads for almost 1,200 miles and driving on nothing but rock, the Meloons and other travelers found it difficult to make 300 miles a day. Highway officials had set fifty miles per hour as the maximum speed. Long hours of daylight, into the wee hours of the morning, caused other problems. It was hard to know when to stop, and sleep seemed next to impossible.

"Even a good, respectable goat wouldn't be seen on this road," Ralph Meloon said.

Traveling conditions worsened as they drove farther north. Heavy rains added to their difficulties. They found no showers or baths along the road, so cleanliness came only be means of occasional warm springs. Gas prices zoomed higher and higher the farther they traveled, peaking at about sixty-five cents a gallon at a time when half that price was the norm back home. Service stations appeared about 100 miles apart, and the rough roads played havoc with tires. Sharp rocks and gravel proved the worst obstacles. The Meloons bought five tires during the 17,000-mile trip.

To relieve the monotony of the journey, the boatbuilding wanderers composed a song that made up in feeling what it lacked in poetry.

"Going up the Alcan, making fifty miles a tire; when the rocks began to fly; sitting in our Chevy, with our hand on the wheel and choking to death on the dust."

The dust was so thick at times that the travelers had to stop the car until it slackened.

"We soon learned," Ralph Meloon said, "it was more fun planning the trip than taking it. It was an ordeal. Anticipation is greater than the reality in everything we do except going to heaven."

The Florida travelers learned the first rule of the Alcan Highway: survival means cooperation—everybody helping everyone else. They found many willing helpers along the way, and they, too, stopped to help when they saw a need.

Ralph called home every day on the trip until they reached White Horse, Yukon. Because it usually took two hours or more to complete each call, he told his mother he would not call again until they had gone to Anchorage and returned to the forty-eight States. But his mother had forgotten that message. As a result, family and friends became concerned when no contact was made for several days.

Ralph, Jr., meanwhile, had befriended a drunken Indian, playfully shoved him, then had run for the car as the man chased him. The lad did manage to reach the car and lock himself in. Ralph's wife, Betty, wrote a postcard home with the disturbing message: "A drunk Indian is trying to get into the car."

That cryptic word caused alarm at home, especially with no other contact for two weeks. The senior Meloons sent Walt after them, convinced by this time that some real harm had come to their loved ones. They also instigated an all-night church prayer meeting in their living room. They would trust God together for some word from the "lost" family.

Ralph remembered telling his mother not to expect a call from him until he had returned to the forty-eight States, but he suddenly felt a strong inner tug to call home. He had no reason but the divine urging, but he knew he must obey the voice of the Lord.

This time the connection was made quickly. A stunned cousin, Lyman Hall, answered the phone.

"It's Ralph! It's Ralph!" he shouted. Great rejoicing ensued, as God's timing had brought joy and peace to grieving hearts.

Ralph discovered to his amazement they had already given him and his family up for dead. A reward had been offered for any information about the Ralph Meloons, dead or alive. Even Dad Meloon, the eternal optimist, had told Ralph's married daughter that the traveling son and family were dead. The very night of the special prayer meeting, Ralph's call came.

Walt reached Chicago on his journey to find the missing family. An inner voice also told him to call home. Ralph's call had come a short time earlier, and Walt breathed praise to God for answered prayer.

The Ralph Meloons continued on their journey southward, heading home. When they reached southern California, they learned they had just missed heavy, damaging floods in which several people had lost their lives. The rest of the trip home proved uneventful.

Seven years later, when Dad Meloon's health began to

slip, the Ralph Meloons again took the trip to Yukon, with Ralph's mother and ailing father along this time. Road conditions had greatly improved since their earlier trip. The four-week journey centered primarily in Dawson City, where the Meloons saw gold being mined in four different ways: panning, bulldozing, dredging, and hydraulically. The thirst for financial gain made a lasting impression on the travelers.

"That's the way the world is today," Ralph said. "We go to any means trying to get material wealth—risking lives, taking chances."

Within forty miles of Dawson City, one of their tires blew. Only one spare remained, and the Meloons questioned their ability to traverse safely the distance that was left. A time of family prayer convinced them they should turn back and take care of the tire situation a few miles back. Two tires blew during those forty miles, and they never would have made it with just the one spare.

When the traveling Meloons decided to go by ferry from Prince Rupert to Vancouver, British Columbia, instead of by the Alcan, they encountered a problem. Room reservations for the two nights on the ferry were all taken, and a long waiting list seemed to cancel any chances they might have for sleeping quarters. That could prove a real hardship for the senior Meloons.

Dad Meloon appealed to the purser for a room for his wife. The ferry official later reported an accommodation available. But it proved to be a third-tier bunk that Mrs. Meloon could not climb into, so W. C. returned to the long line waiting to talk with the purser. In his friendly way, he began to chat with the woman in front of him.

"It looks rather discouraging," he said to her after he had explained their situation.

"We're trying to get rid of one of our rooms," she

countered. Again, the Lord had made a way for the Meloons.

As they traveled later, back on the rough northwest roads, they discovered that one of the big bumps apparently had dislodged their camp stove and the only spare tire with a rim. That left only one rim, so they had to find the missing one—a seemingly hopeless task after searching for more than an hour.

"Let's pray about it," Dad Meloon said.

In a matter of moments after returning to the bumpiest area, he walked right to the tire.

The three Meloon sons, and their offspring as well, rarely allow the helplessness of a situation to deter them. Their parents' example has made it easier for them to trust God in every situation.

12

Ministry in Bankruptcy

As current president of Correct Craft, Inc., Walt Meloon quite naturally meets the public eye more frequently than do his brothers and other members of their families. But all of them have the opportunity, ability, and willingness to share their faith and make it practical with vivid examples of God's dealing in their lives, both personal and business.

As a Sunday school teacher for many years, Ralph Meloon has had an effective ministry that has touched many lives. A strong defender of the faith, he was one of several Christian leaders called in a few years ago when a denominational school in Florida was under fire. Despite scores of testimonials praising the school, Ralph refused to bend under pressure to soft-pedal his criticism of the institution's liberal stance. He presented several points of contention having to do with school policy and related matters. Though criticized by some for his bold stand, Ralph also met with praise and respect for displaying the courage of his convictions.

Ralph and Betty spend most of their time at the Midwest Correct Craft warehouse distribution center in Angola, Indiana. They began in a log cabin on stilts on small Lime Lake in Indiana. Their living room, dining

An aerial view shows the present Correct Craft plant in
Pine Castle, Florida.

room, kitchen, and office were all in one big room, with
two bedrooms and a bath off to the side. Betty typed and
did most of the other office work. She also washed their
laundry on the porch in an old wringer machine.

They now have purchased several lovely acres on
Crooked Lake, where they have built a warehouse and a
residence, although they still have a house in Pine Castle which they call home. Betty now has time to do the
gardening and sewing she loves, but she is ready to help
in the office when needed. She also travels with Ralph
to boat shows and on other business trips. Their son
Ken, twenty-seven, and his wife and child live nearby.
He is president of Midwest Correct Craft, and his
brother, Ralph, Jr., is president of the West Coast Correct
Craft in Sacramento, California.

Walt has had nationwide contacts in Christian Business Men's Committees and a warm friendship with evangelist Billy Graham and members of his team. An exploding ministry has resulted, and it seems to be growing daily. It has puzzled as well as humbled him.

"Surely you don't want a businessman who has entered into bankruptcy in the pulpit," he responds to invitations to speak. But the demand seems to be increasing.

When the field chairman of The Evangelical Alliance Mission (TEAM) invited Walt to visit their missionaries in West Irian, Indonesia, and speak to them for ten days, the Correct Craft executive first balked at the idea. What could he say to a group of dedicated missionaries that would really help them, especially for such an extended period? He decided to put out a fleece to be sure the Lord really wanted him to go.

"Lord," he prayed, "if You're really in this, if You want me to go to West Irian, seal it by giving me someone to introduce to You."

A young man by the name of Steve Yetter was just about to leave Correct Craft to enter the air force. Walt asked him if he had a New Testament. Receiving a negative reply, Walt invited him to stop by his office and pick one up.

When Steve walked into the executive's office, Walt opened up his New Testament. Then he turned to John 3:16.

"Steve," he said, "I want you to read this."

The young man read it aloud.

"Are you a Christian?" Walt asked.

"Yes," Steve responded, "I'm a Presbyterian."

"When did Christ come into your heart?"

Steve hesitated, groping for an answer.

Walt invited him to read the verse again.

"Substitute your own name for 'the world,'" he suggested.

Steve complied, then followed along as Walt read to him Romans 10:9-10, "That if thou shalt confess with thy mouth the Lord Jesus, and shalt believe in thine heart that God hath raised him from the dead, thou shalt be saved. For with the heart man believeth unto righteousness; and with the mouth confession is made unto salvation."

Walt looked him squarely in the eyes.

"Steve," he said, "wouldn't you like to settle that right now?"

The lad nodded without a moment's hesitation.

"Yes, sir," he said.

"All right, Steve," Walt suggested, "I'll pray and you pray after me. 'Lord, I'm a sinner. I know it, and I need to be saved from my sin. I want to receive Your Son, Jesus Christ, as my personal Saviour.'"

Phrase by phrase, the young man uttered the prayer.

"Now, what happened to you?" Walt asked.

"Jesus came into my heart and saved me," Steve responded.

Walt pressed the matter further.

"I want you to write in the flyleaf of your Testament, 'I received Jesus Christ into my heart this afternoon in Mr. Meloon's office.' When Satan gets after you while you're in the air force, just pull this out and remind him whose property you are."

The transaction completed, and with a spiritually renewed Steve Yetter on his way to the air force, Walt Meloon suddenly realized a decision had been made for him.

"OK, Lord," he said, "I'm ready to go to West Irian.

81

But how in the world does a layman like me go to the mission field on faith? People will look at me and figure I don't need any help financially since I'm a layman."

The Reverend Richard Harvey, a pioneer leader in the Youth For Christ movement before becoming a pastor and later southeastern district superintendent for the Christian and Missionary Alliance, arrived in the area for meetings. Walt confronted him with the problem.

"Do like I've done," Harvey suggested. "When it comes time to go, borrow any money you will need from the bank. Tell them you'll pay it back when the Lord sends the money in."

Walt Meloon set up a fund and waited to see what might happen. When it came time to buy his ticket, he had only $28 in the fund, so he borrowed money for ninety days. Just as he prepared to leave for West Irian, money began to come into the special fund. Gospel Volunteers, a project of Gordon Purdy and Camp of the Woods in New York, officially voted to send Walt out so that gifts might be given through them.

Meloon mentioned his forthcoming trip in conversation with his car dealer one day. A few days later, the dealer called Walt at his office.

"I have a little check for your trip," he said. "I want to 'make a few points up there.'"

"Now, Charlie," Walt began to remonstrate before he was interrupted.

"I know, Walt, that's not the way you make points up there!" His check followed shortly thereafter.

Walter Bennett, Chicago advertising executive who handles the Billy Graham Evangelistic Association account, contributed generously. Other gifts in varying amounts came from Orlando insurance executive Don Mott, one of the Correct Craft distributorships in New

Jersey, and many others. (About three months after Walt returned from West Irian, one of the airlines notified him they had overcharged for part of the flight. The check they sent him equaled the interest on both notes, which had already been paid off!)

One of Walt's first tests on arriving in Hong Kong came with the sad news that the comptroller of Correct Craft, Ray White, a warm personal friend, had died suddenly. Walt, Jr., convinced him by overseas phone that Ray would want him to stay and complete his assignment on the field.

Walt Meloon's favorite text, which he employs as a launching pad for most of his messages, is Proverbs 3:5-6: "Trust in the LORD with all thine heart; and lean not unto thine own understanding. In all thy ways acknowledge him, and he shall direct thy paths."

Even as he pondered over these verses, Walt found himself praying. "Lord," he said, "I just don't have a message."

That same clear inner voice that had led him in the past now quietly thundered its message: "Tell the story of your bankruptcy." Walt could not understand the wisdom of relating that kind of message to a group of missionaries, but the voice persisted.

After his first message, Meloon found himself being questioned at the dining table. TEAM was losing its hospital on the south coast of West Irian, where the building was being washed into the sea. They needed $50,000 to move and rebuild it. And the Lord knew this was exactly the message they needed. Walt had repeated one statement a number of times: "God is not poor." That became the rallying cry of the missionaries and their leaders in subsequent business sessions.

In between his times of public ministry, in which he

always elaborated on the one theme, Meloon spent the days talking and praying with missionaries. They decided to trust God for the $50,000. In the next two years, they received $100,000.

Walt Meloon's ministry in bankruptcy appeals both to the masses and to individuals. A Connecticut man came to the boat show in New York so that he could talk with Walt about his financial woes. He was on the verge of declaring bankruptcy.

"Why do you want to get out from under this pressure?" Meloon asked him. "If it's simply to ease your burden, that's not reason enough. You must be willing to let God and others know that you're more interested in bringing honor and glory to the Lord Jesus Christ than anything else."

In his public ministry, Walt zeroes in on the subject of bankruptcy. "You may say that God doesn't deal in dollars and cents," he begins, "but I will dispute it. He has done it all through the years. A Christian cannot make a decision of any kind that is not spiritual.

"God has used bankruptcy ever since the Garden of Eden. There was bankruptcy with Adam and Eve, not in dollars and cents, but total bankruptcy when Cain killed Abel. That was a bankruptcy of discipline to do God's will. David faced bankruptcy time and time again. Moses, when he killed the Egyptian, had to run for the desert. All of their experiences had the same elements as those found in financial bankruptcy.

"Divorce is nothing in the world but a form of bankruptcy—a bankruptcy of love and affection that we should never run out of. I believe God wants to handle all bankruptcy in the same way."

After a chance meeting and a time of sharing experiences, Dr. V. Raymond Edman, then president of

Wheaton College in Illinois, started sending Walt his books, one at a time. "I went through all of them carefully, and studied the problems he faced and how he went about solving them," Walt says. "Especially do I remember the plaque that graced his wall: 'It's always too soon to quit.' I wish Christians everywhere could remember that."

In 1955, TEAM missionary candidates Bob and Doris Frazier had expressed a need for a boat in their work in West Irian.

"How near is someone with the necessary equipment to maintain such a boat?" Walt asked them. Without waiting for a reply, he suggested that the Fraziers spend several months in Titusville and make it their home while they learned firsthand how to build and maintain boats.

TEAM missionaries Bob and Doris Frazier lived part-time in this houseboat for seven years in West Irian, Indonesia. Other missionaries lived on it while building permanent homes along a river.

Some weeks later, the Fraziers showed up at the Correct Craft plant. The Meloons found them a place to live, and they worked together on a $15,000 boat which was made available to the missionaries at half price. (They lived on the boat for most of seven and a half years while serving the Lord in West Irian. Most of TEAM's eleven mission stations on the south coast were opened and serviced by the boat.)

But only three weeks before their departure time for the field, the Fraziers learned that a mere $2,300 of the needed $7,500 had come in through TEAM for the boat. They expressed concern to the Meloons.

"We began this on faith," Walt said, "and the Lord will see us through." Then he thought of a possible approach. "Where are the churches that support you?"

Bob Frazier mentioned churches in North Carolina, South Carolina, and Virginia.

"Get on the phone," Walt suggested. "Call the people in each of those places. Tell them you'll have the boat in front of their church on a certain date, and you want to hold a missionary rally to thank the Lord for what He has provided. I'll lend you a truck and a driver."

About ten days later, Frazier called Walt and shouted excitedly, "God has sent in all the money we need! Your driver is on the way back with all his expenses paid."

The Meloon brothers are the kind of men who "grow" on others. The longer one knows Harold, Ralph, and Walt, the more he realizes their willingness and ability to help. Their friendliness evidences itself in many ways.

Asked to describe her sons, Mrs. Meloon said, "They are three wonderful Christian men who would go anywhere and do anything to help someone. They are unselfish with their time, their money, and themselves, just as I prayed they would be before they were born."

An engine manufacturer in South Carolina invoiced Correct Craft much lower than the Meloons expected on one occasion.

"You seem to have shorted yourself about $1,400," they informed the firm's manager. "We called to find out how we can pay you back."

"No," came the response. "We got the engines from

Walt Meloon presented a gift to Dayuma, an Auca Indian, in 1959 at the Wycliffe Bible Translators' guesthouse in Quito, Ecuador, when he went to South America with Dr. Cameron Townsend, Wycliffe director.

Ford at a low cost just before they raised the prices. We wanted to pass the savings on to you. But we sure appreciate your calling about this."

Walt's travels and ministry with the Billy Graham crusades have taken him to Honolulu, Malaysia, Bali and other places in Indonesia, Singapore, Australia and New Zealand. Industrial and lay audiences, in particular, relate well to his message. Ann, his wife and traveling companion, is a forceful though quiet power for good in his life. Many physical problems have plagued her throughout much of her married life, but she says, "It's good when you know you're not going in your own strength."

Willingness to "stay by the stuff" and keep things going at the plant while Walt is being used elsewhere are admirable traits of character in the lives of the other Meloons and the rest of the Correct Craft force as well. Walt feels that they too are sharing, and will share, in the spiritual rewards for whatever is accomplished in his extensive speaking ministry. Some tension has existed between the brothers at times because of Walt's frequent travels, but the situation is more harmonious today than ever before and is steadily improving.

Walt and Ann Meloon first met Billy and Ruth Graham in 1942 when Don and Faye Mott invited them for Thanksgiving dinner in Orlando "to meet a young pastor and his wife [the Grahams] from Chicago to help organize Youth For Christ locally." That began a warm and growing friendship.

Today Walt is a licensed worker with the Christian and Missionary Alliance, and in 1974 he and Paul Milburn, president of Alliance Men, had a fruitful ministry to laymen in the Philippines, commended highly by C&MA President Dr. Nathan Bailey and Foreign Secretary Dr. Louis L. King. Meloon has been active in Alliance Men for several years, first as southeastern president, then as international president in 1975.

In 1972, while attending a board meeting of Gospel Volunteers in New York, Walt and Ann sat next to a New Jersey couple, Ernie and Ruth Jones, new Christians. When the Meloons were introduced to them, they responded almost in unison, "We have one of your boats! Wasn't there an article about you in *Power?*"

"Yes," they replied, and for three days the Meloons sat and talked and prayed with the Joneses who were teetering on the verge of bankruptcy. The couple, in turn, passed on the exciting Correct Craft story to Richard H. Schneider, senior editor of *Guideposts*, who, with his wife, was present at a later meeting in New Jersey.

A few weeks later, the Schneiders came to Orlando for two days and spent many hours with the Meloons. The result was an article about the boatbuilders in the November 1973 issue of *Guideposts*, which shared the Meloon story with many thousands.

In a letter to Walt some time later, Dick Schneider wrote: "Give a special handshake to your dad, from whom such a wonderful light emanates. Just being in his presence seems to do something for one." W. C. Meloon had suffered a stroke in 1965 that left him partially incapacitated, especially in his speech, but the glow still remained. He had not had an active part in the company since his stroke. Mrs. Meloon is on the board of directors and still maintains a vital interest in all that goes on with the business.

The Meloons' philosophy might well be summed up in a statement often made by Walt: "If there is no crisis, there is no need for faith in God."

13

Sowing Good Seed

Most believers consider personal witnessing as a planned program that is desirable but optional. The Meloons have a philosophy of sharing their faith that is nonthreatening to all concerned. It simply becomes a natural part of themselves, an overflow of the life of Christ who dwells within.

Walt Meloon explains it in a way that young and old alike can understand and any believer can undertake. "All you need to do," he tells any inquirer, "is to put down on paper what happened to you when you were saved. Then go out tomorrow; and, during your normal contacts of the day, tell others what you wrote on the paper."

Meloon suggests a first important step to help a person get started. "Have you ever told your spouse what happened to you when you were saved? If not, do it tomorrow morning at the breakfast table. Then you'll find yourself sharing the same thing later in the day with a friend, your neighbor, and others. This is how witnessing starts: by doing."

The Meloons first realized their responsibility as witnesses when they became active in Christian Business Men's Committee work and began to attend CBMCI conventions.

"The thing that fired me up," Walt said, "was people like Leon Sullivan, a Philadelphia investment executive who talked everywhere about Jesus to all kinds of people—waitresses, maids, bellboys, service station attendants.

"I used to think it was enough to be a church usher or deacon," he added, "but it was a new revelation to me that God had given us a commission to tell this one thing: how wonderful Jesus is and what He has done for me."

The Reverend O. G. Hall had once challenged Walt to be God's businessman. The boatman fought the idea, but he could never get away from it. He recalls the first time he heard a message on the Gadarene demoniac as told in Mark 5.

"Suddenly I realized Jesus asked him to go and tell what had happened, not to remain for further instruction, nor to have Jesus or someone else go with him, but to go and share."

The Meloons also believe in the principle of earning the right to witness to others by displaying friendliness and concern. This is seen often in their dealings with their employees at Correct Craft.

When one of their workers, Johnny Burrell, needed a place to stay, Dad Meloon told him he could room with them for awhile. Johnny had a drinking problem about which Dad reasoned, argued, and prayed with him often. Even though the senior boatbuilder was president of the Temperance League and active with the organization, he forgave Johnny time and time again, always giving him another chance to redeem himself.

Later, Johnny left and was gone for some time. The Meloons went on a trip, and while they were away, Johnny came back to die of tuberculosis. Dad Meloon wept many tears of regret that he had not been there to help Johnny Burrell in his last hour of need. That same tenderness of spirit carried over into his business dealings.

Every effort has been made to repay past debts, though they are not legally due. Showing concern for their creditors, the Meloons have found ways to pay back funds which otherwise would have been lost during the chapter 11 settlement.

When the firm needed electrical work done in 1974, Louis Christensen of Johnson Electric Company submitted an estimate of $4,300 for the job.

"Take it back to your office," the Meloons told their former creditor, "and make it $6,300. Then we'll sign it."

Correct Craft no longer makes fifty-foot motor yachts like this one shown on Indian River at Titusville, since the company changed to smaller and fiberglass boats.

92

"What's that for?" Christensen asked.

"This will make up for some of the loss you incurred during the chapter 11 experience."

Another creditor wanted to buy a boat from the Meloons. Walt pulled out from his desk drawer a piece of paper showing amounts creditors had forgiven Correct Craft. The boatbuilders owed the would-be purchaser $1,100.

"We'll take $1,100 off the original price," Walt said "and the boat's yours."

The Meloons heard about still another creditor, a widow who was bedridden with illness and almost destitute. They repaid all she had forgiven under the bankruptcy laws. As she lay motionless, her arthritic body racked with pain, the widow wept.

"I never lost faith the money would be paid," she said.

Torry Mosvold, biggest Correct Craft creditor, accepted about one-third of the company's stock offered by the Meloons to repay him.

Correct Craft has retained cordial relations with their former creditors, attesting to the integrity of the boatbuilding Meloons and adding to the authenticity of their witness.

The real joy of being in the boat business, the Meloons will tell you, is to be able to supply utilitarian craft to missionaries in strategic areas of the world. In recent years, they have given four boats to World Vision missionaries, two to TEAM, and four to the Christian and Missionary Alliance, so their joy has been full.

But to be able to display such generosity, of course, they must merchandise a worthy product that sells on the commercial market. This they have done for fifty years.

Correct Craft has manufactured dozens of models at

Seven Correct Craft boats are hauled at one time.

one time or another. Today the firm produces only fifteen models, ranging from the sixteen-foot Skier Inboard to the twenty-four-foot San Juan Inboard/Inboard-Outboard Soft Ride V-Hull Fly Bridge.

An issue of the *Orlando Tribune*, the firm's unique house organ, might describe some of these boats in technical detail, alongside a Billy Graham sermon and an inspirational poem. More than 100,000 readers have enjoyed the commercial-spiritual potpourri, as evidenced by hundreds of letters they have written to the editors.

A two-page picture spread in one issue bore the banner headline: "Walt Meloon and Correct Craft Entertain Native Indians from Colombia, South America." A subhead spelled out the rest of the story: "Wycliffe Bible translators responsible for bringing these guests to U.S. from their native home at the headwaters of the Amazon River."

Because the spiritual emphasis seems such a natural part of the Meloon organization, readers seldom if ever protest the interspersing of "inspirational" material with commercial. Knowing the Meloons, as most of them do, they do not consider the mixture objectionable.

The Correct Craft boat, then, as pictured and described in the *Orlando Tribune*, is a simple yet complex vessel, a tool for the missionary and a pleasure provider for believer and unbeliever alike.

Retired boat designer Adam Ingram served as plant chaplain for eight years until his retirement in 1974. He had a most effective ministry. During the company's Christmas dinner in 1968, Ingram engaged the man sitting next to him in conversation. The employee heard about the real meaning of Christmas, and before the dinner was over he had professed faith in Jesus Christ.

Ingram's fervor and fruitfulness resulted from a little-known secret in his life. At 3:00 o'clock every morning, for half an hour, he and his wife sought divine guidance for the day. God answered their prayers, and it never seemed to surprise them. At 6:30 A.M. the Ingrams arose for their normal day's activities.

Careful to observe proper business protocol, Ingram looked for opportunities and invitations to visit in the homes of employees. Christian film showings every other Thursday at the Correct Craft plant, with noncompulsory attendance, opened many doors which Ingram tactfully entered.

One such experience took the chaplain and his wife

into one of central Florida's more dangerous areas to visit an employee in his home. Earlier, Ingram and his wife had given the man a New Testament. Now the young man's parents wanted to know more about the new religion their son believed.

Their mission completed, the Ingrams returned to their home. The very next evening, a soldier just back from Vietnam was the victim of a meaningless killing in the same area they had visited. But their early-morning encounter with the Lord had prepared the way for their safety. They thanked God again for His continued faithful protection as they went about His business.

Harvesttime does not always come at the time of contact. One day Walt Meloon opened a letter while his brother Ralph responded to a call from the switchboard operator to see a man who had come to visit him.

When the two brothers had finished their appointed tasks, they met again to resume discussion of company business. But first they had more important matters to share.

Walt's letter had come from a man who had worked at Correct Craft for only a few months.

"I hated everything about the place," he wrote, though the majority of workers at the plant seem to enjoy its wholesome atmosphere. "I was under conviction after seeing the films and hearing testimonies. Finally, I became so angry one day that I walked off the job and headed for Ohio."

A few nights after arriving in a small town in the Buckeye State, the vagabond employee found himself walking aimlessly down the street. A familiar sound —the singing of a hymn—floated to his ears as he passed a little church. He entered the sanctuary and later responded to the invitation to receive the Saviour.

"Now that I'm a Christian," he wrote, "I want you to forgive me for the things I thought and said—and stole. I want to repay you for the things I took."

A few days later a money order for $100 came to Correct Craft as the first repayment.

Ralph rejoiced with Walt in the good news his letter contained, then he described the experience he had enjoyed with his visitor. The man had worked for Correct Craft fifteen years earlier. He too had become irritated at the Christian witness maintained at the plant and had vented his wrath by maliciously sawing some of the company's best plywood and mahogany into small pieces. Then Ralph, instead of rebuking the man, had shared his personal testimony with him.

As he stomped out of Ralph's office, the man offered a

Adaptability became a Correct Craft trademark as they built chests (foot lockers) for military use during World War II.

parting sarcastic shot. "If I ever need Jesus Christ," he snarled, "you'll be the first to know!"

Now he was fulfilling that promise. The night before, he had trusted Christ in a little church.

Many businessmen get all their enjoyment from mushrooming sales and accelerating profits. The Meloons find joy in hearing of God's faithfulness in the lives of others.

14

Some Other Meloons

To avoid confusion with the name Walter, which has been widely used in the Meloon family, someone came up with a nickname for the son of President Walter O. Meloon and his wife, Ann. "Little Walt," as Walter Nathaniel Meloon is inappropriately called, is the strapping six-foot-four-inch vice-president and general manager of the firm, father of Walter Gary, twelve, and Lori Ann, ten. He is married to the former Barbara Burns.

Born in 1937, Walt, Jr. (as he is also known by some, though not properly), moved to Titusville with his parents in the early 1940s. One of his earliest recollections is of preschool days and dredging on the lakes with his father and grandfather. Thus when Dr. E. J. Daniels, Southern Baptist evangelist, came to have dinner with the Meloons one day Little Walt came up to him after the meal had been completed and asked, "Do you want to go 'drudging' with us?"

Young Walt majored in mischief through several of his formative years. Red Tucker, who worked for the Meloons for many years, painted the outsides of boats for Correct Craft, while six-year-old Walt, Jr., was allowed to paint the insides. When Red's face appeared in front of him one day on the job, Walt, Jr., dutifully painted it. Red retaliated by spraying him thoroughly.

The younger Meloon recalls traveling often three or four times a day between Pine Castle and Titusville, while his dad tried to keep up with operations at both plants.

"We were about the only ones who had gas coupons during those war years," Little Walt said, "so we saw very little traffic. I can remember Dad coming home with a bent fender from hitting a cow, for there was often more livestock on the road than cars.

"Dad would get up very early in the morning," he continued, "and put a wooden bed in place of the rumble seat on our old 1936 Ford, which was used as a family car and truck. This made a bed so we could catch up on our sleep as we rode. We carried palm fronds to keep off the masses of black mosquitoes.

"Because of food rationing, we raised our own chickens. They became almost a staple diet for us. Before the war was over, we preferred plain beans and bread. Too much of a good thing is too much!"

Walt, Jr., recalls cutting his leg badly one day when the family lived in Indian River City. "Mother had to take me to the doctor," he said, "and while stitching me he accidentally stuck me with his scissors. My proper reflex action sent one of my new cowboy boots right into the doctor's mouth. Fortunately for me, he took it graciously."

Walt, Jr., remembers his grandfather Meloon as a man who acted on impulse. "One Thanksgiving he decided he wanted every Correct Craft family to have a turkey. He went out and bought a truckload of the fowl, then distributed them to some three-hundred employees at the Titusville and Pine Castle plants."

When Walt, Jr., was fourteen, the plant had just built two forty-two-foot cruisers. When one of the craft sprang a gas leak and exploded, his father suffered a severe burn on his arm and was rushed to a hospital in the city of Cocoa. Newspaper reporters and photographers descended upon the Meloon home and harassed the lad's mother. Rising to the occasion, despite his youthful years, Walt, Jr., managed to squelch the newsmen and send them on their way.

He remembers receiving Christ as his Saviour at the little Baptist church in Titusville, under the ministry of the Reverend Ben Hall, and today he is active in church work. Five years under the Christian influence of Hampden-DuBose Academy in Zellwood, Florida, helped to prepare him for his time of decision.

Little Walt's fun-loving Uncle Harold, unknown beyond his own bailiwick, has retained fond memories of a dad who believed in working early and late, and loved to work with his hands. He remembers, too, his father's straightforward, often courageous, business dealings.

"Three different men in the insurance business had tried unsuccessfully to obtain performance bonding for Correct Craft," Harold recalls. "Dad had always said, 'You can handle your own business better than anyone else.' So he went to New York City to see the bonding man personally.

"Dad boldly presented his case," Harold continued. "He also corrected some of the inaccuracies that had been presented earlier. The rule was that they couldn't handle more than one-third of the bonding needed. When Dad got through his presentation, the maximum bonding was approved and by noon it was sold out.

Dad's courage, integrity, sincerity, and prayer saved the day."

In 1972, when Mrs. W. C. Meloon underwent a cataract operation, Harold and his two brothers took turns caring for their father, a semiinvalid since his stroke in 1965.

Harold started flying a glider at the age of twelve.

"We used to have wonderful times barnstorming all over the country," he said. "All of us flew the primary glider behind high-speed boats, even Dad."

By the time he was seventeen, Harold was handling a crew of men in Winter Park as they put retaining walls down through the canal system. Like his brothers, he learned valuable lessons of discipline and work at a younger age than most men.

All officers of Correct Craft, Inc. in 1975 were Meloons: chairman of the board, Ralph C. Meloon; president-treasurer, Walter O. Meloon; vice-president and general manager, Walter N. Meloon; acting secretary, Mrs. W. C. (Marion) Meloon. Ralph Meloon, Jr., also serves on the board as a director.

Other directors include Otis Jackson, James S. Welch, Gordon Purdy, Dave Chambers, Russell Hovde, and Torry Mosvold.

President Walter O. Meloon and Ann also have a daughter, Mrs. Robert (Etta) Warner, whose husband is manager of Correct Craft's New England warehouse in Rochester, New Hampshire.

Ralph Meloon, Jr., is president of West Coast Correct Craft in Carmichael, California, and his sister, Marian Abel, lives in Brockton, Massachusetts, with her husband.

Harold and his wife, Jewel, have four children. Shirley lives in Conway Acres, Florida, with her one child.

She works for Hammond Electronics in Orlando. Harold, Jr., lives in Milton, New Hampshire, where he works for a rubber company that makes dashboards for cars. Daniel and Steve work in sales at the plant in Pine Castle. Their cousin, David, son of Don, works in the same department.

W. C. Meloon once described his purpose in business. "Correct Craft exists only as a means for the Meloon family to be in the Lord's business," he said.

His wife, sons, and other members of the family have subscribed to the same goal. With that as their aim, the boatbuilding Meloons have experienced success. No one today questions their preoccupation with the Lord's business, even when the boat business continues to waver between prosperity and peril.

15

A Meloon Gets His Hearing Back

On September 5, 1974, W. C. Meloon—*barely able to get about*—began to experience severe pains in the region of his heart. For the first time in his eighty years, he asked for a doctor. His wife quickly called Walt, Jr., who summoned the fire department's rescue squad and accompanied them as they sped to the hospital.

Emergency personnel at Orange Memorial Hospital placed the senior Meloon in intensive care. Mrs. Meloon, still sharp and alert, phoned Walt in New Hampshire and Ralph in Indiana.

"The doctor says you'd better come home right away if you want to see Dad alive," she told them.

Early next morning, Ralph kept an important appointment 125 miles from the Angola, Indiana, plant. Then he and Betty flew home to Pine Castle. Ralph visited his father several times during the next day and a half, a painful experience because of his dad's labored breathing and failure to recognize him.

Walt and Ann, meanwhile, left New Hampshire by car early Saturday morning and drove all that day and the next. Four different times during the long trip home the car radio gave out Billy Graham's "Hour of Decision" message on the subject of angels. They rejoiced in its timeliness as they traveled the seemingly endless miles.

Late Sunday night, September 8, Walt and Ann drove into Pine Castle. Next morning they went to the hospital. Walt experienced the same distressed feeling Ralph had as his father continued to breathe heavily and showed no signs of recognition.

At about 9:30 Monday evening, Walt left the hospital. His father's condition remained unchanged. Walt, Jr., had left his phone number at the hospital so his grandmother would not need to be disturbed. A call came to him at home around 1:30 A.M.

"Dad," came the solemn voice, "the doctor called a couple of minutes ago. Grandad's gone."

Walt's first reaction was to withhold the news from his mother until morning. He called Ralph to share the news. Moments later, he called his brother again.

"Mother has every right to know now," he said. "Can you meet me there in twenty minutes?"

Harold already was spending the night at his mother's, and soon the three sons awakened her. They told her the news.

"So soon?" she asked with a wistful trace of surprise.

The four who had been closest to the senior Meloon down through the years now gathered in the living room. They rehearsed God's blessing through a husband and father, recalling experiences both familiar and unfamiliar to the others. Two hours passed like moments as they shared together, their eyes glistening with unshed tears.

They remembered their loved one's day-by-day commitment and walk that seldom faltered, a shining example of obedience, a strength of character that refused to listen to anyone else being criticized.

"We'll sure miss him," Mother Meloon said for them all, "but we do not wish him back. He's far better off with the Lord he loved and served."

Ralph reflected on the fact it was election day in the county. Nervous, exhausted candidates had to wait until the end of the day to know the results; Dad's election was sure.

Marion Meloon spent much of the day cleaning her apartment, lining closet shelves, and tidying every nook and cranny. At eighty-two, she still drove a car and did her own shopping. Because of the earlier cataract operation, she wore both glasses and contact lenses.

Friends of Walt and Ann summed up the funeral. "How blessed was that wonderful service," they wrote. "It was a worship service to God's praise and glory."

Grandson Ken recalled that the only tears at Grandpa's funeral were those of joy. Each of the three sons spoke briefly at the funeral service, recalling their dad's influence upon their lives.

One friend who had lost his own father earlier wrote the Meloons, "I particularly understand how you feel at this point. Your dad was my first employer and helped me out when I was decidedly in need as a teenager. I'll never forget him."

With remarkable similarity, long-time Correct Craft employees wrote or spoke of the senior Meloon as a fair and just man who would not ask anyone else to do a job he was not willing to do himself, a man willing to give counsel and encouragement at any time, the kind of man you felt free to go to, a fair man, a thoroughly honest man, a man who really loved the Lord and his fellowman.

Proud grandchildren recalled a priceless heritage. "Grandpa used the boat business as an opportunity to witness for the Lord Jesus Christ," Ken Meloon said. "There was no difference to him between the sacred and the secular; it was all sacred."

A nephew wrote Mrs. Meloon shortly after the funeral service: "A truly great spirit warmed the personality that was your husband so many long and good years. I shall always remember his ready smile, his deep concern and energetic reaction toward those things that are really worthwhile in life."

Torry Mosvold wrote words of wisdom: "Let's learn a little bit from him and let us always do like him—be quiet, nice and pleasant with everybody and most of all have a good testimony about our Lord and Saviour."

16

Labor and Rest

The boatbuilding Meloons have a work philosophy best illustrated by Walt in a portion of his article published in 1973:

> Did you hear the story about the man who inherited a million dollars?
>
> Instead of going to work the next morning, he stayed home to enjoy the luxury of his new affluence.
>
> He went outside to get his morning newspaper, but there was no paper.
>
> While he waited for it, he decided to turn on the sprinkler and water his lawn. A turn of the faucet brought forth no water.
>
> "Well, I'll just go in and have breakfast while I wait," he said to himself, still not really irritated by his frustrations.
>
> On plugging in the coffee maker, he found no electricity. He hurried out of the house and called to his neighbor in the next yard.
>
> "I have no newspaper, there is no water, and the electricity is off!" he yelled over the fence.
>
> "Haven't you heard?" his neighbor replied. "Everyone inherited a million dollars yesterday."
>
> God planned for people to work for many reasons. Labor is necessary to accomplish anything, be it building boats—my work—or whatever your work is.

Labor is also a means of supporting ourselves and our families. We have neither the skills nor the resources to provide everything necessary for life. By the skills we do have we earn money with which to buy the necessities which others by their skills can produce.

Labor makes the day worthwhile. Physical labor is most beneficial to mankind, not only because of what it produces but because of what it does for health. The hardest working people I know are the healthiest and happiest.

Recently I was discussing with a judge the possibility of a thirty-hour week. In that judge's opinion if we reduce the workweek to thirty hours, every jail in the country would have to be expanded.

During the summer I had breakfast with two young men, one of whom is the son of a very famous preacher. Those two young men, while traveling abroad, had found a little fourteen-bed mission hospital urgently in need of enlargement.

The boys had no extra money, but they offered their labor. Their faces glowed as they told me how they had worked fourteen and sixteen hours a day in the hot desert sun, leaving blood and skin on rocks and mortar boxes as they helped to expand that hospital to accommodate sixty patients so that the missionaries could extend their witness.

God has much to say about labor, and He places great importance on it. He Himself labored six days to complete the earth and the heavens. "Thus the heavens and the earth were finished, and all the host of them" (Gen 2:1).

But He also set aside one day in seven as a day of rest. "On the seventh day God ended his work which he had made; and he rested on the seventh day from all his work which he had made" (v. 2).

God kept a balance by resting from His labor the

seventh day. It is just as important to rest and regain strength as it is to labor the six days.

Today we are in danger because we want the fruits of labor without the labor itself. And conversely, we are ignoring God's command for one day of rest in seven.

Walt Meloon then recounted his firm's experience during World War II, when the seventh day was devoted to the Lord, regardless of pressure to do otherwise.

"Labor and rest," his article concluded, "God's formula for balanced living. Blessed is the man or woman who observes both."

America's inflation-ridden businessman in the late '70s needs an answer to his problems. The Meloons feel they have discovered that solution in the testing fires of experience.

"A businessman has no business being in business just to make money," Walt Meloon says. "Every businessman automatically is in danger of making money his god. Whenever he makes a decision in favor of his business as opposed to accepting an opportunity or obligation to witness for the Lord Jesus Christ, he has made money his god, for the moment, at least. He is favoring mammon, and his priorities are mixed.

"It is impossible to overemphasize the importance of right priorities, especially in the business world, though these priorities apply to the life of every believer.

"Advice not to mix Christianity and business is heresy of the worst kind," he concludes. "A man's business, whatever it might be, ought to be an integrated and integral part of his Christianity. It either complements or opposes his spiritual stance."

A true "chip off the old block," Walt Meloon thus